MW01175126

49 Days of Prayer
with Gospel of Luke

by

Keith D. Walker

Published by

Turning Point
GLOBAL

Calgary, Saskatoon, Kingston, Wellington, NZ
ISBN: 978-1-387-96284-6

ISBN 978-1-387-96284-6 90000

9 781387 962846

Pelican Landing at Emma Lake Picture by Great Friend: Bryan Roset
Picture on back cover is Keith dancing with his daughter, Gillian Tillman, at her wedding
Copies of this book may be ordered from:
Amazon.com, Amazon.ca or Lulu.com

Acknowledgements

I am grateful to God for the gift of Viv, my beautiful wife and best. Together we acknowledge, with gratefulness, the profound influence of our children, extended family, friends and colleagues on us. We have been blessed with an excellent community of co-journeyers over the years. God is Good.

Keith D. Walker
June 2019
Saskatoon
KeithDWalker.ca

Introduction to this Resource

As I've said elsewhere, I have a deep longing that you no doubt share with me. I desperately want the notice and attention of God. I want to hear Him, to be heard and to be present with Him. We have one life to live. We can live this life independently and naturally or naturally with the invited supernatural presence of God. Given the original design of God for humankind, given God's amazing grace and love, and given God's willingness – I choose to walk with God and seek to develop a transforming relationship with Him.

This book is a derivative book, from other prayer books I've assembled, for my own use. I do hope it might be likewise useful to you. It is a book of 49 daily prayers continues to help my expressions of dependence on God, my renewed, and constantly refreshing devotion to Him. The prayer prompts at the end of the book are intended to help me more systematically intercede. It is just as natural to forget as it is to remember!

From time to time it is good to be reminded into whose presence we come when we pray. The attributes of God galvinize my focus on the Lord Jesus Christ's magnificience and infinite worthiness. He is superior, supreme, and so undescribably great; whereas I am small. Yet, He loves me and invites me to meet with Him, to walk and talk with Him along life's way. May I be ever mindful of Who it is that I bow before, as I pray.

Creator and Redeemer, I worship You as the infinite,[1] omnipresent,[2] omnipotent,[3] omniscient,[4] wise,[5] providential,[6] immutable,[7] sovereign,[8] incomprehensible[9] God of the Bible. You are accessible,[10]

---

[1] 1 Kings 8:22–27; Jeremiah 23:24

[2] Psalms 139:7–12; Jeremiah 23:24; 1 Kings 8:27.

[3] Genesis 18:14; Revelations 19:6; Matthew 19:26

[4] Psalms 139:2–6; Isaiah 40:13–14; 66:1; Psalms 90:2; 102:12; 139:7-10; 145:3; 147:5; Hebrews 4:13; Romans 11:34; 1 Kings 8:27; Jeremiah 23:23, 24; Acts 17:27, 28; Job 11:7-10; 1 John 3:20; Romans 16:27; 1 Kings 8:29; Psalm 139:1-16; Isaiah 46:10; Ezekiel 11:5; Acts 15:18; John 21:17; Hebrews 4:13

[5] Proverbs 3:19; 1 Timothy 1:17; Romans 11:33; I Corinthians 2:7; Ephesians 1:6, 12, 14; Colossians 1:16

[6] Acts 17:25

[7] Hebrews 1:10–12; 13:8; James 1:17; Malachi 3:6; Hebrews 6:17; Numbers 23:19; Psalms 33:11; 102:27; James 1:17

[8] Isaiah 46:9–11; Genesis 50:20; Acts 2:23

[9] Job 11:7–19; Romans 11:33

simple,[11] one,[12] triune,[13] spirit,[14] self-existent[15] and self-sufficient,[16] immanent,[17] transcendent,[18] eternal,[19] and immense.[20] You are the jealous[21] God of wrath.[22] You are holy,[23] impeccable,[24] righteous[25] just,[26] true,[27] faithful,[28] longsuffering,[29] good,[30] merciful,[31] gracious,[32] and loving.[33] All that You will do and have done and everything about You is worthy.[34] I worship You in the beauty of Your perfections.

[10] Deuteronomy 4:7. Psalm 27:4; Matthew 6:6; John 14:6; Ephesians 2:13; 3:12; Hebrews 4:16; 7:25; 10:22; James 4:8

[11] The simplicity of God means that God is a unified being – that He is one essence

[12] Mark 12:29; Ephesians 4:6; Deuteronomy 6:4–5; Isaiah 44:6–8

[13] 1 John 5:7; Matthew 28:19; 2 Corinthians 13:14

[14] John 4:24

[15] Exodus 3:13–14; Psalms 33:11; 115:3; Isaiah 40:18 ff.; Daniel 4:35; John 5:26; Romans 11:33-36; Acts 17:25; Revelations 4:11.

[16] Psalms 50:10–12; Acts 17:25; the aseity of God

[17] Acts 17:28

[18] Isaiah 57:15

[19] Deuteronomy 33:27; Psalm 90:2; Psalm 90:2; 1 Timothy 1:17

[20] Isaiah 40:28; 1 Kings 8:27

[21] Exodus 20:5-6

[22] Exodus 15:7; Deuteronomy 9:19; Psalm 69:24; John 3:36

[23] Leviticus 19:2; 1 Peter 1:15; Exodus 15:11; Isaiah 57:15; Isaiah 6:3; Revelation 4:8

[24] Hebrews 6:18

[25] Romans 1:17

[26] Psalms 119:137; 99:4; Isaiah 33:22; Romans 1:32

[27] John 17:3; Titus 1:1–2; Numbers 23:19; I Corinthians 1:9; II Timothy 2:13; Hebrews 10:23; Titus 1:2

[28] Deuteronomy 7:9; Psalms 89:1–2

[29] Romans 2:4; 9:22; I Peter 3:20; II Peter 3:16

[30] Psalms 107:8; 36:6; 104:21; 145:8, 9, 16; Matthew 5:45; Acts 14:17

[31] Psalms 103:8–17; Nehemiah 9:17b

[32] Psalms 111:4; 1 Peter 5:10; Ephesians 1:6, 7; 2:7-9; Titus 2:11; Exodus 34:5-6; 1 Peter 2:2, 3; God has compassion, is slow to anger and is pardoning.

[33] John 3:16; Romans 5:8; Luke 1:64, 72, 78; Romans 15:9; 9:16, 18; Ephesians 2:4; 1 John 4:16

[34] Romans 11:22; the omni-benevolence of God

William Temple said it so well: "To worship is to quicken the conscience by the holiness of God, to feed the mind with the truth of God, to purge the imagination by the beauty of God, to open the heart to the love of God, to devote the will to the purpose of God."[35] Of course, worship involves awareness of God, awe in His presence, and adoration of Him. We are in awe because of the revelation of His inexhaustible excellences and acts of creation and redemption. Worship is our affirmation of His supreme and exclusive worthiness, through our humble praise of all He is and does.[36] Nehemiah and author of Hebrews said it this way: Stand up and bless the LORD your God forever and ever! Blessed be Your glorious Name, which is exalted above all blessing and praise! You alone are the LORD; You have made heaven, the heaven of heavens, with all their host, the earth and everything on it, the seas and all that is in them, and You preserve them all. The host of heaven worships You. Through Christ then, let us continually offer up a sacrifice of praise to God, that is, the fruit of the lips that give thanks to His Name.[37]

For me, prayer is about connecting with my Creator, Redeemer, Healer, Sanctifier, and Transforming Friend. The first sections of this book focus on the magnificence of Christ, the names of God and the attributes of God. After reminding myself of who God is then prayer can be the safe place where I can be honest and where I can say "Your will be done, O LORD." Most of this book consists of prayers inspired by the later half of the Gospel of Luke. Ideally a person might read the Scripture passages, as I have done and find the prayers a form of response to the Gospel passage (Lectio Divina or "divine reading"). Of course, prayer is a platform for us to bring concerns, petitions, supplications, and to engage God's workings in my life and in the lives of others. Prayer is the space I open up to my heavenly Father to walk with Him and talk with Him along life's way – for He cares deeply for me. I know he wants my attention, even more than I want His. He calls out to me, saying:

---

[35] William Temple. I still recall when Viv and I discovered this insightful description of worship, in a order of service booklet in Salisbury Cathedral, Salisbury, UK. These five elements delineated by William Temple have since helped me frame the elemental aspects of worship.

[36] Vernon Grounds and Leslie Flynn

[37] Nehemiah 9:5, 6 and Heb. 13:15

[38] The brilliant group - Naturally 7 wrote these vocal play lyrics (above). I think these beautifully capture the heart of God's desire to fellowship with me, and with you. This is His open invitation to find a place to BE with Him, as He is with me.

Say you love Me; tell me that you love Me. Say that I am the One that you'll come running to; to hold you through the rain. Say you love Me and there is no one else above Me. Open up your heart to Me; I'll always be – all you'll ever need. Say you love Me.[38]

Saint Luke

Saint Luke by Guido Reni

Luke was born in Antioch (Syria), as a Greek. He was the writer of the Gospel and the Acts of the Apostles; the only Gentile to have written a book in the Bible. Luke (called "the Evangelist") may have been born a slave and educated to be a resident family physician. He was the beloved physician[39] and is considered by some to be the patron of physicians and surgeons. His writings were based on his connections with Paul and his companions (i.e., Theophilus).[40] Saint Luke had a great knowledge of the Septuagint and of all things Jewish. Luke's Gospel is longer than St. Matthew's and his two books are as long as all 14 of St. Paul's Epistles. Luke remained with Paul during his final imprisonment.[41] Six of Jesus' miracles and eighteen of His parables are only found in Luke's Gospel. He joined Paul at Troas (51 AD)[42] and accompanied him into Macedonia (travelling to Samothrace, Neapolis, and Philippi). Luke left Philippi to rejoin Paul in Troas (58 AD) and they travelled together through Miletus (Tyre, Caesarea) to Jerusalem.[43] Luke stayed with Paul when he is imprisoned in Rome (61 AD).[44] Luke's life after Paul's death is uncertain. Some claim he was martyred and others say he lived a long life (perhaps dying at 84 in Greece).

---

[39] Colossians 4:14; Paul, Eusebius, Saint Jerome, Saint Irenaeus and Caius, all refer to Luke as a physician

[40] Luke 1:1-3

[41] 2 Timothy 4:11

[42] Acts 16:8-10 (note change to "we" language)

[43] Acts 20:5 (note change to "we" language)

[44] Philemon 24

49 Days of Prayers with the Gospel of Luke

Dear Lord, I ask that you would ease the pounding of my heart by the quieting of my mind as I come to You. Interupt the complexities, confusion and messiness of this day with Your calmness and peace. Release the tension of my nerves and muscles with the soothing music of my whole body, mind, will and emotions touching You and all You have done to enliven me. At the end of this day, help me to know the restoring and refreshing power that comes with the gift of sleep. Through the night and for the benefit of my day, teach me the art of taking two minute vacations that come with permission to pause from the scurry and hurry: To delight in conversations with friend and strangers; and to hug, to hold, to smile, to let others go first, to sit with eyes closed and hum the first stanza of a favourite chorus or give thanks for the people in my life. Slow me down, deepen my appreciations, and cause me to overflow with expressions gratitude. May I give much more attention to what is working than what is not. Dear Lord Jesus Christ, use the sense of Your presence and use the cover of night to slow me down and teach me to not be in such a hurry.

Gospel Reading: Luke 11:1-13

It happened that while Jesus was praying in a certain place, after He finished, one of His disciples said to Him, "Lord, teach us to pray just as John also taught his disciples." [2]He said to them, "When you pray, say: 'Father, hallowed be Your name. Your kingdom come.[3]'Give us each day our daily bread. [4]"And forgive us our sins, For we ourselves also forgive everyone who is indebted to us who has offended or wronged us. And lead us not into temptation but rescue us from evil.'" [5]Then He said to them, "Suppose one of you has a friend, and goes to him at midnight and says, 'Friend, lend me three loaves of bread; [6]for a friend of mine who is on a journey has just come to *visit* me, and I have nothing to serve him'; [7]and from inside he answers, 'Do not bother me; the door has already been shut and my children and I are in bed; I cannot get up and give you *anything*.' [8]I tell you, even though he will not get up and give him *anything just* because he is his friend, yet because of his persistence *and* boldness he will get up and give him whatever he needs. [9]"So I say to you, ask *and* keep on asking, and it will be given to you; seek *and* keep on seeking, and you will find; knock *and* keep on knocking, and the door will be opened to you. [10]For everyone who keeps on asking persistently, receives; and he who keeps on seeking, finds; and to him who keeps on knocking persistently, the door will be opened. [11]What father among you, if his son asks for a fish, will give him a snake instead of a fish? [12]Or if he asks for an egg, will give him a scorpion? [13]If you, then, being sinful by nature, know how to give good gifts to your children, how much more will your heavenly Father give the Holy Spirit to those who ask *and* continue to ask Him!"

☐ ☐ ☐ ☐ ☐ ☐ ☐ ☐ (1)

Lord please teach me to pray.[45] Lord teach me to be generous and to give both out of my abundance and with sacrifice, according to the needs I see and the promptings of Your Holy Spirit. You have said, *ask and it will be given to you; seek and you will find; knock and the door will be open*

to you. Today I ask, I seek and I knock, please hear my prayer and give me good gifts from Your loving heart. Thank You for the gift of the Holy Spirit who lives in me, as Comforter, Guide, and Friend. May the transformation and sanctifying work of the Holy Spirit continue to renew and refresh me, mold me, melt me and

[45] Inspired by Luke 11:1-13

make me, more and more each day, like Jesus Christ. I thank You Triune God, Father, Son and Spirit for Your incredible love. Thank you Jesus for bringing me this far. In Your light I see the light of my life. Your teaching is brief and to the point: You persuade me to trust in my heavenly Father; You ask me to fullly love You; and You command me to love others. What is easier than to believe in God? What is sweeter than to love You? Your yoke is pleasant; Your burden is light. You are the One and only Teacher! You promise everything to those who obey Your teaching. Thank You Jesus, now and always. Amen.[46]

Lord God of Heaven, who has so lavishly blessed me, and those I love; keep us humble. Forgive my boasting pride, and help me to share what You have given. Impress me with a sense of responsibility, and remind me, that one day a reckoning will be required of me. Sanctify my love of my family and friends. Set apart and bless the causes that occupy me, that my boasting may be turned into humility and my pride into a ministry to people everywhere. Make me Your chosen channel of blessing. Make my circle of influence Your own through my living as an ambassador of reconciliation and a peace-maker in the lives of others. Help me make an impact on this world for Jesus Christ, for I ask this in His holy Name. Amen.[47]

Gracious Father, I pray to You for Your holy Catholic Church. Fill Her with Your truth. Keep Her in Your peace. Where She is corrupt, reform Her. Where She is in error, correct Her. Where She is right, defend Her. Where She is in want, provide for Her. Where She is divided, reunite Her; for the sake of Your Son, my Saviour Jesus Christ. Amen.[48] Lord, teach me to be generous, teach me to serve You as I should, to give and not to count the cost, to fight and not to heed the wounds, to toil and not to seek for rest, to labour and ask not for reward, except to know that I do Your holy will.[49]

O Lord, grant that I greet this coming day in peace. Help me in all things to rely upon Your holy will. In every hour of the day reveal Your will and unfolding plan to me. Bless my dealings with all who surround me. Teach me to treat all who come to me throughout the day with gentleness. In all my deeds and words guide my thoughts and feelings. In unforeseen events let me not forget that all are sent or permitted by You. Teach me to act firmly and wisely, without

---

[46] Nicholas of Cusa (1401-1464)

[47] Adapted from Peter Marshall (1902–67)

[48] William Laud (1573-1645)

[49] St. Ignatius of Loyola (16th Century)

embittering and embarrassing others.
Give me strength to bear the fatigue of
the coming day with all that it brings.[50]

Almighty Father govern the
hearts and minds of those in authority
and bring the families of the nations
who are divided and torn apart by the
ravages of sin into subjection to Your
just and gentle rule. You are alive and
reign in unity, one God, now and
forever.[51] O Lord my God, great,
eternal, wonderful in glory, who keeps
covenant and promise for those who
love You, You are the life of all, the
help of those who flee to You, and the
hope of those who cry to You. Please
cleanse me from my sins, and from
every thought displeasing to You.
Cleanse my soul and body, my heart
and conscience that with a pure heart
and a clear mind, with perfect love and
calm hope, that I may venture
confidently and fearlessly into
tomorrow and the days to follow.[52]

---

[50] Philarat

[51] Reflections for Daily Prayer

[52] Saint Basil

Gospel Reading: Luke 11:14-28

And at another time Jesus was casting out a demon who was controlling a man so as to make him mute; when the demon had gone out, the mute man spoke. And the crowds were awed. [15]But some of them said, "He drives out demons by the power of Beelzebul (Satan), the ruler of the demons." [16]Others, trying to test Him, were demanding of Him a sign from heaven. [17]But He, *well* aware of their thoughts *and* purpose, said to them, "Every kingdom divided against itself is doomed to destruction; and a house *divided* against itself falls. [18]If Satan also is divided against himself, how will his kingdom stand *and* continue to survive? For you are saying that I drive out demons by the power of Beelzebul. [19]Now if I drive out the demons by Beelzebul, by whom do your sons, the Jewish exorcists, drive them out? For this reason they will be your judges. [20]But if I drive out the demons by the finger of God, then the kingdom of God has already come upon you. [21]When the strong man, fully armed, guards his own house, his belongings are undisturbed *and* secure. [22]But when someone stronger than he attacks and overpowers him, he robs him of all his armor on which he had relied and divides his goods as spoil. [23]He who does not believe in Me, as Lord and Savior, is against Me because there is no impartial position; and he who does not gather with Me by assisting in My ministry, scatters. [24]"When the unclean spirit comes out of a person, it roams through waterless places in search of a place of rest; and not finding any, it says, 'I will go back to the person from whom I came.' [25]And when it comes, it finds the place swept and put in order. [26]Then it goes and brings seven other spirits more evil than itself, and they go into the person and live there; and the last state of that person becomes worse than the first." [27]Now while Jesus was saying these things, one of the women in the crowd raised her voice and said to Him, "Blessed is the womb that gave birth to You and the breasts at which You nursed!" [28]But He said, "On the contrary, blessed are those who hear the word of God and continually observe it."

☐ ☐ ☐ ☐ ☐ ☐ ☐ ☐ (2)

Good evening Heavenly Father, good evening Lord Jesus, good evening Holy Spirit, good evening Triune God.

Heavenly Father I worship You as the Creator and Sustainer of the universe. Lord Jesus, I worship You, as Saviour and Lord. Holy Spirit, I worship You, as Sanctifier of the people of God. Glory to the Father, and to the Son, and to the Holy Spirit. Heavenly Father, I pray that I may live through this night in Your presence and please You, more and more, into tomorrow. Lord Jesus Christ, I pray that in this day and tomorrow I may take up my cross and follow You. Holy Spirit, I pray that You will fill me with Yourself and cause Your fruit to ripen in my life: love, joy, peace, patience, kindness, goodness, faithfulness, gentleness, and self-control. Holy, blessed and glorious Trinity, three persons in one God, have mercy upon me. Amen.[53]

O Lord, hear; O Lord forgive. O Lord, listen and act and do not delay.[54] I thank You, Lord Jesus, that all authority in heaven and earth is Yours. You are Ruler, Master and King. Your kingdom come on earth as it is in heaven. I know that the evil one, Satan, and his cohorts are defeated and that You are infinitely more powerful than powers and principalities of the air. I pledge my allegiance this evening to the Triune God: Father, Son and Holy Spirit. I determine, by Your grace, to hear the Word of God and obey it. Fill me afresh with Your Spirit and displace any distracting attachments I have with flesh, the world or with evil so that I may be completely Yours. I am with You and need You. I desire with all my heart to serve You, for Jesus' sake and in His mighty Name I pray.

Watch me, dear Lord, with those who wake, or watch, or weep tonight, and give Your angels charge over those who sleep. Tend Your sick one, Lord Christ. Rest Your weary ones. Bless Your dying ones. Soothe Your suffering ones. Pity Your afflicted ones. Shield Your joyous ones. And all, for Your love's sake. Amen.[55] You are from everlasting to everlasting O Lord. I turn my thoughts to You as the hours of darkness and of sleep begin. O Sun of my soul, I rejoice to know that all night I will be under the unsleeping eye of One who dwells in eternal light. To Your care, O Father, I now commend my body and my soul. All day You have watched over me and Your companionship has filled my heart with peace. Give me sound and refreshing sleep. Give me safety from all perils. Give me in my sleep freedom from restless dreams. Give me control of my thoughts, if I should lie awake. Give me wisdom to remember that the night was made for sleeping, and not for the harbouring of

[53] John Stott

[54] Daniel 9:19

[55] St. Augustine (4th Century)

anxious or fretful or shameful thoughts.

Give me grace, if as I lie in bed I think at all, to think upon You. My soul shall be satisfied and my mouth shall praise You with joyful lips as I remember You and meditate on You in the night. To Your care also, O Father, I would commend my friends and family, asking You to keep them safe and to be present in their hearts tonight, as their loving Spirit of restfulness. I pray also for the wider circle of all my associates, my fellow workers, my fellow citizens and even those strange to me, but dear to You, through Jesus Christ our common Lord. Amen.[56]

God of surprises, when I think You are not present in my life, You reveal Yourself in the love of friends and family and nurture me in Your never-ending affection. God of surprises, when I think You are not present in our community, You labour to make us of one heart and cause us to share gladly and generously. God of surprises, when people think You are not present in our world, You bring hope out of despair and create growth out of difficulty. God of surprises, You are ever with us. When the days go by and my vision fades, keep surprising me. When my hope dims

and my patience wears thin, keep coming to me. Teach me to keep my lamp lit and to be prepared, that I may see Your loving presence among us.[57]

Heavenly Lord, You long for the world's salvation: stir me from my apathy, restrain me from excess and revive in me new hope that all creation will one day be healed in Jesus Christ our Lord.[58]

---

[56] Adapted from John Baillie, 1949

[57] Francis Brienen

[58] Reflections for Daily Prayer

Gospel Reading: Luke 11:29-36

Now as the crowds were increasing in number, He began to say, "This present generation is a wicked generation; it seeks an attesting miracle as a sign, but no sign will be given to it except the sign of Jonah, the prophet. ³⁰For just as Jonah became a sign to the people of Nineveh, so will the Son of Man also be a sign to this generation. ³¹The Queen of the kingdom of Sheba will rise up in the judgment with the men of this generation and condemn them, because she came from the ends of the earth to listen to the wisdom of Solomon, and look, something greater than Solomon is here. ³²The men of Nineveh will stand up as witnesses at the judgment with this generation and condemn it, because they repented at the preaching of Jonah, and look, something greater than Jonah is here. ³³"No one lights a lamp and then puts it in a cellar nor under a basket to hide the light, but instead it is put on the lampstand, so that those who come in may see the light. ³⁴The eye is the lamp of your body. When your eye is clear and spiritually perceptive, in a way focused on God, your whole body also is full of light and benefits from God's precepts. But when it is spiritually blind, your body also is full of darkness and devoid of God's word. ³⁵Be careful, therefore, that the light that is in you is not darkness. ³⁶So if your whole body is illuminated, with no dark part, it will be entirely bright with light, as when the lamp gives you light with its bright rays.

 (3)

Lord, You are a gracious and compassionate God, slow to anger and abounding in love, a God who relents from sending calamity.[59] In my distress I called out to You and You answered me. From the depths of the grave I called for help, and You listened to my cry . . . You brought my life out of the pit. O Lord my God, when my life was ebbing away I remembered You. Lord, and my prayers rose to You to Your holy temple. Those who cling to worthless idols, forfeit the grace that could be theirs. But I, with a song of thanksgiving, will sacrifice to You. What I have vowed I will make good. Salvation comes from the Lord.[60]

Our Father, as I come into Your presence this evening, I thank You for the hope You have given me that there

---

[59] Jonah 4:2

[60] Jonah 2:2; 6b-9

is victory in Jesus over death and that nothing can separate me from Your love. Almighty Father of the universe, I come to You, conscious of my own shortcomings, but with confidence and composure, knowing that having put my trust in You this night, my faith is well-founded. May I tolerate nothing in my personal living that weakens Your testimony and my witness in the world. Teach me that no country is better than its citizens, and no stronger than those in whom it puts its trust. Grant to those who have positions of authority and responsibility that they would humble themselves before You and be just. How they, and how I need You Lord. So use them and use me, guide us and act through us, I ask in Jesus' Name and for His sake. Amen.[61]

Enable me, O God, to collect and compose my thoughts before an immediate approach to You in prayer. May I be careful to have my mind in order when I take upon myself the honour to speak to the Sovereign Lord of the universe, remembering that upon the temper of my soul depends, in very great measure, my success. You are infinitely too great to be trifled with, too wise to be imposed on by my mock devotion, and You abhor a sacrifice without a heart. Help me to entertain an habitual sense of Your perfections and presence, as an admirable help against cold and formal performances that I am sure to display without Your living fully in and through me. Save me from engaging in rash and presumptuous prayers and from abrupt breaking away to follow impulses of business or pleasure as though I have no need to pray or, in arrogance, feel I have no need of You.[62]

Lord I want to walk with those who walk in the light, who know and experience Your grace and live as a full participant in the kingdom of the day. Dispell the darkness and fill me with Your light. Be, Lord Jesus, a bright flame before me, a guiding star above me, a smooth path below me, a kindly shepherd behind me: Today, tonight, and forever.[63] Almighty Lord God, Your glory cannot be approached, Your compassion knows no bounds, and Your love for all humankind is beyond expression. In Your mercy guide me to the haven of Your will and make me truly obedient to Your commandments, that I may not feel ashamed when I come before the Messiah's judgement seat. For you, O God, are good and everloving, and I glorify You, Father, Son and Holy

---

[61] Adapted from Peter Marshall (1902–67)

[62] Susanna Wesley, 1669-1742

[63] St. Columba (6th Century)

Spirit, now and forever, to the ages of ages.[64]

O God my Father, let me not be content to wait and see what will happen, but give me the determination to make the right things happen. While time is running out, save me from the false patience which is akin to cowardice. Give me the courage to be either hot or cold, to stand for something, lest I fall for anything, in Jesus' Name, Amen.[65]

All glorious God, I give You thanks. In Your Son, Jesus Christ, You have given me every spiritual blessing in the heavenly realms. You chose me, before the world was made. You adopted me as Your child in Christ. You have set me free by His blood and You have forgiven my sins. You have made known Your purpose: to bring heaven and earth into unity in Christ. You have given me Your Holy Spirit, the seal and pledge of my inheritance.[66] All praise and glory be Yours, O God, for the richness of Your grace, for the splendour of Your gifts, and for the wonder of Your love.[67]

---

[64] Orthodox Liturgy

[65] Peter Marshall Prayer used in the Senate, 10 March 1948

[66] Inspired by Ephesians Epistle

[67] Desmond Tutu

Gospel Reading: Luke 11:37-54

Now after Jesus had spoken, a Pharisee asked Him to have lunch with him. He went into the Pharisee's home and reclined *at the table* without ceremonially washing His hands. [38]The Pharisee noticed this and was surprised that Jesus did not first ceremonially wash before the meal. [39]But the Lord said to him, "Now you Pharisees clean the outside of the cup and plate, as required by tradition; but inside you are full of greed and wickedness. [40]You foolish ones act without reflection or intelligence! Did not He who made the outside make the inside also? [41]But give that which is within as charity, acts of mercy and compassion, rather than as a public display; but as an expression of your faithfulness to God, and then indeed all things are clean for you. [42]"But judgment is coming to you Pharisees, because you self-righteously tithe mint and rue and every little garden herb, tending to all the minutiae, and yet disregard *and* neglect justice and the love of God; but these are the things you should have done, without neglecting the others. [43]Woe to you Pharisees, because you love the best seats in the synagogues and to be respectfully greeted in the market places. [44]Woe to you! For you are like graves which are unmarked, and people walk over them without being aware of it and are ceremonially unclean." [45]One of the lawyers who was an expert in the Mosaic Law answered Him, "Teacher, by saying this, You insult us too!" [46]But He said, "Woe to you lawyers as well, because you weigh men down with the burdens of man-made rules which are unreasonable requirements and hard to bear. You, yourselves, will not even touch the burdens with one of your fingers to lighten the load. [47]Woe to you! For you repair *or* build tombs for the prophets, and it was your fathers who killed them. [48]So you are witnesses and approve the deeds of your fathers, because they actually killed them, and you repair *or* build their tombs. [49]For this reason also the wisdom of God said in the Scriptures, 'I will send them prophets and apostles, some of whom they will put to death and some they will persecute, [50]so that charges may be brought against this generation, holding them responsible, for the blood of all the prophets shed since the foundation of the world, [51]from the blood of Abel to the blood of Zechariah, the priest, who was murdered between the altar and the house *of God*. Yes, I tell you, charges will be brought against this generation.' [52]Woe to you lawyers, because you have taken away the key to knowledge. You yourselves did not enter, and you held back those who were entering by your flawed interpretation of God's word and your man-made tradition." [53]When He left there, the scribes and the Pharisees began to be very hostile toward Him and to interrogate Him on many subjects, [54]plotting against Him to catch *Him* in something He might say.

 (4)

What can I say to You, my God? Shall I collect together all the words that praise Your holy Name? Shall I give You all the names of this world, You, the Unnameable? Shall I call you God of my life, meaning of my existence, hallowing of my acts, my journey's end, bitterness of my bitter hours, home of my loneliness, You my most treasured happiness? Shall I say: Creator, Sustainer, Pardoner, Near One, Distant One, Incomprehensible One, God both of flowers and stars, God of the gentle wind and of terrible battles, Wisdom, Power, Loyalty and Truthfulness, Eternity and Infinity, You the All-merciful, You the Just One, You are Love itself?[68] O Lord my God, most merciful, most secret, most present, most constant, yet changing all things, never new and never old, ever in action, yet ever quiet, creating, upholding, and perfecting all; who has anything but Your gift? Or what can any person say when speaking of You? Yet have mercy upon me, O Lord, that I may speak to You, and praise Your Name.[69]

Lord I wish to be wise, not foolish; to be clothed with Your righteousness and not be greedy, or wicked. I want to be a just and loving person who is attentive to the poor for their sake, not for my own reputation. I desire to be clean in heart and conscience from the inside-out. Lord please help me to be a person of integrity. Lord help me to be a listener, a burden-bearer and a facilitator of faith, truth, love, justice and hope, for Your kingdom sake.

O Lord of the night, to whom all the stars are obedient, in this hour of darkness I, too, submit my will to You. From the stirrings of self-will within my heart, from cowardly avoidance of necessary duty, from rebellious shrinking from necessary suffering, from discontentment with my lot, from jealousy of those whose lot is easier, from thinking lightly of the one talent You have given me, because You have not given me five or ten, from uncreaturely pride, from undisciplined thought, from

---

[68] Karl Rahner

[69] Jeremy Taylor, 1613-67 (based on Augustine, 354-430)

unwillingness to learn and unreadiness to serve - O God, set me free. O God my Father, You are often closest to me when I am farthest from You and You are near at hand even when I feel that You have forsaken me, mercifully grant that the defeat of my self-will may be the triumph in me of Your eternal purpose. You have accepted my invitations to be with me. May I be an excellent host. Make my heart Your home. May I know who I am in You. May I grow more sure of Your reality and power. May I attain a clearer mind as to the meaning of my life on earth. May I strengthen my hold upon life eternal. May I look more and more to things unseen. May my desires grow less unruly and my imaginations more pure. May my love for my fellow humans grow deeper and more tender, and may I be more willing to take their burdens upon myself. To Your care, O God, I commend my soul and the souls of all whom I love and who love me, through Jesus Christ our Lord. Amen.[70]

Father, I yearn for a better understanding of spiritual things. Give to me clear vision that I may know where to stand and what to stand for. I know I must stand for something, lest I fall for anything. Remind me, O God, that You have not resigned or retired but You are active and intimately connected and attentive to my comings and goings. Harassed and troubled by the difficulties and uncertainties of the hour, I rest my mind on You, the one who does not change. Lord Jesus, help me to see clearly that the pace at which I am living these days shuts You out of my mind and heart, and leaves me, even with good intentions, to wander in the misty land of half-truth and compromise. Deliver me, O God, from the God-helps-those-who-help-themselves philosophy, which is really my cloak for sheer unbelief in Your ability and willingness to take care of me and my affairs, for Jesus' sake. Amen.[71]

O God, just before I sleep, I remember before You all the people I love, and now in the silence I say their names to You . . . All the people who are sad and lonely, old and forgotten, poor, and hungry and cold, in pain of body and in distress of mind. Bless all who especially need Your blessing. Make this a good night for me. This I ask for Your love's sake. Amen.[72]

[70] Adapted from John Baillie, 1949

[71] Adapted from Peter Marshall (1902–67)

[72] William Barclay

Gospel Reading: Luke 12:1-12

In the meantime, after so many thousands of the people had gathered that they were stepping on one another, Jesus began speaking first *of all* to His disciples, "Be *continually* on your guard against the leaven of the Pharisees, their pervasive, corrupting influence and teaching, which is a hypocrisy that produces self-righteousness. [2]But there is nothing so carefully concealed that it will not be revealed, nor so hidden that it will not be made known. [3]For that reason, whatever you have said in the dark will be heard in the light, and what you have whispered behind closed doors will be proclaimed on the housetops. [4]"I say to you, My friends, do not be afraid of those who kill the body and after that have nothing more that they can do. [5]But I will point out to you whom you should fear: fear the One who, after He has killed, has authority *and* power to hurl you into hell; yes, I say to you, stand in great awe of God and fear Him! [6]Are not five sparrows sold for two copper coins? Yet not one of them has ever been forgotten in the presence of God. [7]Indeed the very hairs of your head are all numbered. Do not be afraid; you are far more valuable than many sparrows. [8]"I say to you, whoever declares openly *and* confesses Me before men speaking freely of Me as his Lord, the Son of Man also will declare openly *and* confess him as one of His own before the angels of God. [9]But he who denies Me before men will be denied in the presence of the angels of God. [10]And everyone who speaks a word against the Son of Man, it will be forgiven him; but he who blasphemes against the Holy Spirit; that is, whoever intentionally discredits the Holy Spirit by attributing the authenticating miracles done by Me to Satan, it will not be forgiven him for him there is no forgiveness. [11]When they bring you before the synagogues and the magistrates and the authorities, do not be worried about how you are to defend yourselves or what you are to say; [12]for the Holy Spirit will teach you in that very hour what you ought to say.

☐ ☐ ☐ ☐ ☐ ☐ ☐ (5)

Jehovah-Father, Spirit, Son – You are the mysterious Godhead, Three in One. Before Your throne, as a sinner, I bend; grace, pardon, and life to me extend.[73] O God, I am a sinner; I am sorry for my sin; I am willing to turn from my sin. I receive You, Christ, as Saviour; I confess You as Lord; I want

[73] Edward Cooper, 1770-1833

to follow You, and serve You, in the fellowship of Your Church.[74] Eternal God, I place myself into Your hands. May I walk together, hand in hand, with those I easily love and work with and with those who are harder to live and work with, and in all my actions may Your will be done.[75] God, who became as I am, may I become as You are.[76]

All knowing and loving God continue to put an impulse in me that repells duplicity and hypocrisy in my life; instead, may my representation of my self to the world be authentic and may I be a person of integrity whether seen by others or not. I know You are my audience 24 hours of the day and night. Cleanse my thoughts, my whispers, my teaching and advice, my opinions and expressed preferences. Please give me boldness to speak the truth in love, to prize and proclaim justice, and to speak truth to power. May I speak Your Gospel with both word and deed. Keep me from the fear of other persons who like me have clay feet but intensify my reverence and surrender to the Lordship of You, my God Almighty. Thank You for Your intimate attention to me and the details of my life. May my life, well-lived, boast of Your care for me and

may my respect and attunment to Your will and to Your Word be pleasing to You. Fill me afresh with Your Holy Spirit, O Lord, that I might bear much fruit and glorify You in all I do and all I am, for Jesus Christ's sake.

O God, my Father, I thank You for this day. I thank You for those who have given me guidance, counsel, advice and good example. I thank You for those in whose company the sun shines even in the rain. Thank You for those who bring a smile to my face even when things are grim. I thank You for those in whose company the frightening things are not so alarming and the hard things are not so difficult. I thank You for those whose presence saves me from falling into temptation and enables me to do the right thing. I thank You for those it is a joy to be with, and those in whose company the hours pass by all too quickly. I thank You for happy times and for every happy memory. I thank You for times of failure to keep me humble, and that remind me how much I need You. Most of all I thank You for Jesus Christ, who in the daytime is my friend and my companion and who in the night is my pillow and my peace. Hear my evening thanksgiving for Your love.[77]

---

[74] Billy Graham

[75] Geogre Carey

[76] After William Blake (1757-1827)

---

[77] William Barclay (1907-1978)

You have heard the longings of the meek, O Lord; You will strengthen their hearts, and turn Your ear to their heart's desire.[78] O blessed Jesus, give me stillness of soul in You. Let Your mighty calmness reign in me. Rule me, O King of gentleness, King of peace. Give me control, the great power of self-control: Control over my words, thoughts and actions. From all irritability, lack of meekness, lack of gentleness, dear Lord, deliver me. By Your own deep patience, give me patience. Make me in this and all things more and more like You.[79] God be in my head and in my understanding. God be in my eyes and in my looking. God be in my mouth and in my speaking. God be in my heart and in my thinking. God be at my end and at my departing.[80] Your sovereign power, formed me after Your image and likeness and when like a wandering sheep I strayed, You brought me back to Your fold again. Wide as the world is Your command, vast as eternity Your love; firm as a rock Your truth must stand.[81]

Breathe in me, Holy Spirit, that I may think about what is holy. Move me, Holy Spirit, that I may do what is holy. Attract me, Holy Spirit, that I may love what is holy. Strengthen me, Holy Spirit, that I may guard what is holy. Guard me, Holy Spirit, that I may keep what is holy.[82] O Triune God, I love You!

---

[78] Psalm 10:17

[79] St John of the Cross (1542-1591)

[80] Book of Hours (15th Century)

[81] Adapted from Isaac Watts, 1674-1748

[82] St Augustine of Hippo

Gootel Reading: Luke 12:13-21

Someone from the crowd said to Him, "Teacher, tell my brother to divide the *family* inheritance with me." [14]But He said to him, "Man, who appointed Me a judge or an arbitrator over the two of you?" [15]Then He said to them, "Watch out and guard yourselves against every form of greed; for not even when one has an overflowing abundance does his life consist of *nor* is it derived from his possessions." [16]Then He told them a parable, saying, "There was a rich man whose land was very fertile *and* productive. [17]And he began thinking to himself, 'What shall I do, since I have no place large enough in which to store my crops?' [18]Then he said, 'This is what I will do: I will tear down my storehouses and build larger ones, and I will store all my grain and my goods there. [19]And I will say to my soul, "Soul, you have many good things stored up, enough for many years; rest *and* relax, eat, drink and celebrate continually."' [20]But God said to him, 'You fool! This *very* night your soul is required of you; and *now* who will own all the things you have prepared?' [21]So it is for the one who continues to store up *and* hoard possessions for himself, and is not rich in his relationship toward God.

☐ ☐ ☐ ☐ ☐ ☐ ☐ ☐ (6)

Before the end of the day and in the knowledge of Your steadfast love, Creator of the world, I pray that You that You would keep watch while I sleep. Defend my sight from evil dreams; defend me from fears and terrors of the night; and please tread under foot my deadly foe so that no sinful thought may know.[83]

Unto You, O heavenly Father, be all praise and glory, day by day. You richly fill my life with various blessings: A home to share, family to love, and friends to cherish. You've given me a place to fill and a work to do. I have a green world to live in, blue skies above me, and pure air to breathe. I experience healthy exercise and simple pleasures. I've been blessed with good books to read and many arts to delight in. There is so much that is worth knowing and the skill, science, and technology to know it. I enjoy the peace that passes understanding, from Your indwelling and the faith that looks through death and the hope of a larger life beyond the grave. In Jesus Christ You have

[83] Time to Pray (2006)

done great things for me: making home sweeter and friends dearer, turning sorrow into gladness and converting pain into the soul's victory, robbing death of its sting, robbing sin of its power, making peace more peaceful, joy more joyful and faith and hope more secure. I thank You! Amen.[84]

Lord I live in a world that over-consumes and a world that parties while many are impoverished. Guard my heart from the idols of destruction, from all kinds of greed and from the propensity to collect stuff. Open my eyes to the usefulness of resources to provide food, shelter, medicine, water, education and social services. Let the taxes I pay and the tithes I offer be well spent. Thank You for the stewardship of much and for the call to be a giver rather than a taker. I give under the shadow of your Cross, in the Name of the Giver of givers. Almighty God, by whose mercy my life has continued for another day, I pray that, as my years increase, my sins may not increase. As age advances, let me become more open, more faithful and more trusting in You. And if I become infirm as I grow old, may I not be overwhelmed by self-pity or bitterness.[85]

Help me, O Lord, to be ever conscious of my temporary time on earth. O Lord, You have freed me from the fear of death. You have made the end of my life into the beginning of true life for me. You give rest to my body through sleep, and at an unknown time You will awaken me with the sound of the last trumpet. Eternal God, on You have I depended from my mother's womb. I have loved You with all the strength of my soul. Forgive me and accept my soul into Your hands, spotless and undefiled, as incense in Your sight.[86]

Lord Jesus Christ, fill me, I pray, with Your light that I may reflect Your wondrous glory. So fill me with Your love that I may count nothing too small to do for You, nothing too much to give, and nothing too hard to bear.[87] O God grant me the spirit of love, which does not want to be rewarded, honoured, or esteemed. This I pray for in Your name, for You are Love, in time and eternity.[88] Spirit of fire and truth, Holy Spirit of courage and fortitude, overcome my weakness and cowardice and feed my soul with a rich and insatiable hunger for righteousness. Give me courage and allow me to drink from Your rivers of living water.[89]

[84] Adapted from John Baillie, 1949

[85] Dr. Samuel Johnson (18th Century)

[86] Macrina, 4th century

[87] St Ignatius Loyola (1491-1556)

[88] After William Law (1686-1761)

Lord Jesus, touch my eyes, as You did those of the blind; then I shall see in things that are visible, together with those things which are invisible. Lord Jesus, open my ears, heal my wounds and purify my life, as You did for those who came to You; then I shall hear and perceive what is true amidst the sounds of the world, and I will find wholeness in myself.[90] When I survey the wondrous cross, on which the Prince of Glory died, my richest gain I count but loss, and pour contempt on all my pride. Were the whole realm of nature mine, that were an offering far too small; love so amazing, so divine, demands my soul, my life, my all.[91] I love You Lord!

[89] Benedict Groeschel (Quiet Moments)

[90] After Origen (185-254)

[91] Isaac Watts (1674-1748)

Gospel Reading: Luke 12:22-31

Jesus said to His disciples, "For this reason I tell you, do not worry about your life, as to what you will eat; or about your body, as to what you will wear. [23]For life is more than food, and the body more than clothes. [24]Consider the ravens, for they neither sow seed nor reap the crop; they have no storehouse or barn, and yet God feeds them. How much more valuable are you than the birds! [25]And which of you by worrying can add one hour to his life's span? [26]So if you are not even able to do a very little thing such as that, why are you worried about the rest? [27]Consider the lilies *and* wildflowers, how they grow in the open field. They neither labor nor spin wool to make clothing; yet I tell you, not even Solomon in all his glory *and* splendor dressed himself like one of these. [28]But if this is how God clothes the grass which is in the field today and tomorrow is thrown into the furnace, how much more *will He clothe* you? You of little faith! [29]So as for you, do not seek what you will eat and what you will drink; nor have an anxious *and* unsettled mind. [30]For all the pagan nations of the world greedily seek these things; and your heavenly Father already knows that you need them. [31]But strive for and actively seek His kingdom, and these things will be given to you as well.

 ☐ ☐ ☐ ☐ ☐ ☐ ☐ ☐ (7)

Lord You have set eternity in my heart,[92] I thirst for You. I hear Your words: *who of you by worrying can add a single hour to his or her life.* Yes I do worry. I am anxious. I do get frustrated. So help me Lord to lean not on my own understandings or insights or, even, my own pleasant dispositions but instead, give me the faith to know and to experience You and Your untiring, ever-present, faithfulness in my life. I seek Your kingdom – may Your kingdom come into my life as it is in heaven. Give me this day my daily bread, shelter me, clothe me, equip me, energize and fill me. Mold me, melt me and make me after Your blessed image. Thank You Lord that You can never be out given. You are generous and gracious beyond measure and imagination. I praise You for Your constant care for me.

Come Almighty King. Come Incarnate Word. Come Holy Comforter. Come great One in Three. Help me Your Name to sing. Help me

[92] Ecclesiastes 3:11

to praise. Father all-glorious, over all victorious, come and reign over me, Ancient of Days.[93] O God, the Father of all humankind, I join myself to the great scattered company of those who, in every corner of every land, are now crying out to You in their need. Hear us, O God, and look with mercy upon our many necessities, since You alone are able to satisfy our deepest needs. Especially I commend to Your holy keeping all who tonight are far from home and friends, all who tonight must lie down hungry or cold, all who suffer pain, all who are kept awake by anxiety or suspense, all who are facing danger, and all who must toil or keep watch while others sleep. Give to them all, I pray, such a sense of Your presence as may turn their loneliness into comfort and their trouble into peace. O most loving God, who in the Person of Your Son Jesus Christ expressed Your love to all the world by relieving all manner of suffering and healing all manner of disease. Grant Your blessing to all who in any corner of the world are serving in Christ's Name: All ministers of the gospel of Christ, all social workers, educators, justice workers, emergency care personnel, all international workers, all doctors and nurses who faithfully tend the sick. Accomplish through them Your great purpose of good-will and common good to all peoples. Without discrimination, grant them in their own hearts the joy of Christ's most real presence. And to me also, as I lie down, grant, O gracious Father, the joy of a life surrendered to Christ's service and the peace of sin forgiven, through the power of His Cross. Amen.[94]

O Father, Your power is greater than all powers. O Son, under Your leadership I need not fear anything. O Spirit, under Your protection there is nothing I cannot overcome.[95] Accept my prayers, dear Father, for those who have no one to love them enough to pray for them. Wherever and whoever they are, give them a share of my blessings, and in Your love let them know that they are not forgotten.[96] Lord, remember not only the men and women of good will, but also those of ill will. But, do not remember all of the suffering they have inflicted. Instead remember the fruits we have borne because of this suffering: our fellowship, our loyalty to one another, our humility, our courage, our generosity, and the greatness of heart that has grown from this trouble.[97]

---

[93] Adapted from Whitefield's Leaflet, 1757

[94] Adapted from John Baillie, 1949

[95] Kikuyu Prayer (Kenya)

[96] A Saint Francis Prayer Book

[97] Source unknown (Found in the clothing of a dead child at Ravensbruck concentration camp)

O God of love, I pray that You would give me love: love in my thinking and love in my speaking. Give me, please, love for my neighbours near and far; love for my friends, old and new; love for those with whom I find it hard to bear, and love for those who find it hard to bear with me. Lord give me love for those with whom I work, and love for those with whom I take my ease. May I love in joy, love in sorrow; love in life and love in death; that so at length I may be worthy to dwell with You, who is Eternal Love.[98] Fashion in me, Lord, eyes within my eyes, so that, with new eyes, I may contemplate Your divine sacrifice. Create in me a pure heart, so that, through the power of Your Spirit, I may inhale Your salvation.[99] I breathe in Your love. You are with me now. Oh how I love You!

---

[98] William Temple, 1881-1944

[99] Joseph the Visionary (a Syrian Father of eighth-century Iraq)

Gospel Reading: Luke 12:32-48

Do not be afraid *and* anxious, little flock, for it is your Father's good pleasure to give you the kingdom. ³³"Sell your possessions, show compassion and give donations to the poor. Provide money belts for yourselves that do not wear out, an unfailing *and* inexhaustible treasure in the heavens, where no thief comes near and no moth destroys. ³⁴For where your treasure is, there your heart will be also. "Be dressed and ready for active service, and keep your lamps continuously burning. ³⁶Be like men who are waiting for their master when he returns from the wedding feast, so that when he comes and knocks they may immediately open *the door* for him. ³⁷Blessed are those servants whom the master finds awake *and* watching when he arrives. I assure you *and* most solemnly say to you, he will prepare himself *to serve*, and will have them recline *at the table*, and will come and wait on them. ³⁸Whether he comes in before midnight, or even after midnight, and finds them so prepared and ready, blessed are those *servants*. ³⁹"But be sure of this, that if the head of the house had known at what time the thief was coming, he would have been awake and alert, and would not have allowed his house to be broken into. ⁴⁰You too, be *continually* ready; because the Son of Man is coming at an hour that you do not expect." ⁴¹Peter said, "Lord, are You addressing this parable to disciples, or to everyone else as well?" ⁴²The Lord said, "Who then is the faithful and wise steward of the estate, whom his master will put in charge over his household, to give *his servants* their portion of food at the proper time? ⁴³Happy, prosperous and to be admired is that servant whom his master finds so doing when he arrives. ⁴⁴I assure you *and* most solemnly say to you, he will put him in charge of all his possessions. ⁴⁵But if that servant says in his heart, 'My master is taking his time in coming,' and begins to beat the servants, both men and women, and to eat and drink and get drunk, ⁴⁶the master of that servant will come on a day when he does not expect him and at an hour he does not know, and will cut him in pieces, and assign him a place with the unbelievers. ⁴⁷And that servant who knew his master's will, and yet did not get ready or act in accord with his will, will be beaten with many lashes of the whip, ⁴⁸but the one who did not know it and did things worthy of a beating, will receive only a few lashes. From everyone to whom much has been given, much will be required; and to whom they entrusted much, of him they will ask all the more.

 (8)

Glory to the Triune God in the highest, and on earth peace, good will among all the people. I praise You, I sing to You, I bless You, I glorify You, I worship You, through the Great High Priest. You are the uncaused God. For Your great glory, O heavenly King, O Father Almighty, O Lord God, the Father of Christ, the spotless Lamb, who took away the sin of the world, have mercy on me and hear my prayer. For You are holy; You are the Lord Jesus Christ to whom belongs all glory, all honour, and I worship to You.[100]

Lord Jesus, You have said *do not be afraid*. I thank You for the truth of Your accompaniment which displaces my fear. You are Emmanuel, You are with me in the journey. You have said that *where my treasure is, there will be my heart*. I choose to put my treasures, talents and time in Your hands, for Your disposal and to invest in things eternal. I tell You I want to be at Your bidding and to watch, with readiness, for opportunities to serve You and Your purposes. I say to You this evening that I will drop anything, take on anything, speak or listen to anyone, give up or give anything, or go anywhere You wish. May I hear Your voice: speak clearly to my heart and help me move my feet, according to Your good, perfect and pleasing will. I want to be a wise and faithful steward of all You've given me to manage and lead. I have been entrusted with much; I am grateful. May I be found trustworthy and merit, by Your grace, Your affirming touch and lovingkindness. So help me God.

LORD Jesus, I turn in confidence to You, since You were tempted in all points like I am, and yet You were without sin. Help me, that I might obtain victory over my temptations. I feel ashamed that I have accessed so little power for my life from You, and so often have fallen at the same old hurdles. Sometimes I grow discouraged and I am filled with doubts when I see so little evidence of growth in grace, in faith, and in spiritual perception. I know that I am not what I ought to be; and I know that I am not yet what I will be; but I thank You that I am not what I once was. For whatever progress You have made with me I give You thanks. By Your grace I am kept from despair. Help me to remember that they who wait upon the Lord shall renew their strength. May I wait and be made strong, through You, Jesus Christ, my Lord. Amen.[101]

---

[100] Apostolic Constitutions

[101] Adapted from Peter Marshall (1902–67)

Lord Jesus Christ, You have said that You are the Way, the Truth and the Life. Do not allow me to stray from You, the Way, not to distrust You, the Truth, nor rest in anything other than You, the Life.[102] Father of all humankind, make the roof of my home wide enough for all opinions, oil the door of my home so it opens easily to friends and strangers and set such a table in my house that my whole family may speak kindly and freely around it. O Eternal God, most merciful Lord and gracious Father, You are my guide, the light of my eyes, the joy of my heart, the author of my hope, and the object of my love and worshipping. You relieve all my needs, and determine all my doubts, and are an eternal fountain of blessing, open to all thirsty and weary souls who come and cry to You for mercy and refreshment. Have mercy upon Your servant. Relieve my fears and sorrows, for You alone, O Lord, can do this.[103]

Grant, O Lord, to all who are bereaved, the spirit of faith and courage, that they may have the strength to come with steadfastness, patience and hope. May these be thankful in the remembrance of Your great goodness and in the sure expectation of a joyful reunion in the heavenly places. This I ask in the Name of Jesus Christ my Lord.[104]

While I sleep, O Lord, let my heart not cease to worship You. Fill my sleep with Your presence, while creation itself keeps watch, singing psalms with the angels, and taking up my soul into its prayer of praise.[105] Be present, merciful God, and protect me through the silent hours of this night, so that I, with others who are wearied by the changes and chances of this fleeting world, may rest upon Your eternal changelessness, through Jesus Christ our Lord.[106]

---

[102] Desiderius Erasmus (15th Century)

[103] Jeremy Taylor, 1613-67

[104] Church of Ireland. Book of Common Prayer

[105] St Gregory of Nazianzus (c.330-389)

[106] Leonine Sacramentary

Gospel Reading: Luke 12:49-59

"I have come to cast judgment on the earth; and how I wish that it were already a fire kindled! [50]I have a baptism of great suffering with which to be baptized, and how greatly I am distressed until it is accomplished! [51]Do you suppose that I came to grant peace on earth? No, I tell you, but rather division between believers and unbelievers; [52]for from now on five in one household will be divided over Me, three against two and two against three. [53]They will be divided, father against son and son against father, mother against daughter and daughter against mother, mother-in-law against daughter-in-law and daughter-in-law against mother-in-law." [54]He also said to the crowds, "When you see a cloud rising in the west, you immediately say, 'It is going to rain,' and that is how it turns out. [55]And when you see that a south wind is blowing, you say, 'It will be a hot day,' and it happens. [56]You play-actors and pretenders! You know how to analyze *and* intelligently interpret the appearance of the earth and sky to forecast the weather, but why do you not intelligently interpret this present time? [57]"And why do you not even on your own initiative judge what is right? [58]For while you are going with your opponent at law to appear before a magistrate, on the way make an effort to settle, so that he does not drag you before the judge, and the judge does not rule against you and turn you over to the officer, and the officer does not throw you into prison. [59]I say to you, you absolutely will not get out of there until you have paid the very last cent.

 (9)

Lord this day has been a gift. A great gift from the Giver of great gifts. I am grateful for all I've observed – all I can observe. I am grateful for the nuances, unique experiences, the once only happenings, the faces and stories representing the lives of people I've interacted with. I am so grateful, I open my heart to see – to see the gifts of this day and the ones that will come tomorrow as blessings. May I bless others by my gratefulness.

O Lord Jesus Christ, God of all consolation, whose heart was moved to tears at the grave of Lazarus; look with compassion on all Your children who have suffered loss. Strengthen in them the gift of faith and give to their troubled hearts the light of hope. May they one day be united again, with tears wiped away, in the kingdom of

Your love. For You died and were raised to life with the Father and the Holy Spirit, God, now and for ever.[107] O Lord my God, my one hope, hear me, that weariness may not lessen my will to seek You, that I may seek Your face with an eager heart. My strength and my weakness are in Your hands: preserve the one, and remedy the other. Let me remember You, understand You and love You.[108]

O Father in heaven, who fashioned my limbs to serve and my soul to follow hard after You, with sorrow and contrition of heart I acknowledge before You the faults and failures of the day that is now past. Too long, O Father, have I tried Your patience; too often have I betrayed the sacred trust You have given me to keep. Yet You are still willing that I should come to You in lowliness of heart, as now I do. I ask You to drown my transgressions into the sea of Your infinite love. Forgive my failure to be true even to my own accepted standards. Forgive my self-deception in the face of temptation and forgive my choosing the worst when I know the better. Forgive my blindness to the suffering of others and my slowness to be taught. Forgive my complacence towards wrongs that do not touch my own case and my over-

sensitiveness to those that do. Lord please forgive me. Forgive my slowness to see the good in those I work with and those I serve. Help me to see the evil in myself. Forgive my hardness of heart towards my neighbours' faults and my readiness to make allowance for my own mistakes and mindless acts and attitudes. Create in me a clean heart, O God, and renew a right spirit within me. Cast me not away from Your presence. Restore to me the joy of Your salvation and give me the strength of a willing spirit. Amen.[109]

O Love, O God, who created me, in Your lo[...]

Tonight, bless me with much humility so that I may feel no shame in expressing my need of You – my living God. Forgive the pride that causes me to strut about like a knight in shining armour when I know full well that I am a beggar in tattered rags.[111] O Holy Spirit, Creator blest, come into my heart and take up Your rest. Come with Your grace and heavenly aid to fill my heart. O Comforter, to You I cry, You heavenly gift of God most high; You fount of life, fire of love, and sweet anointing. Praise be to you, Father and Son, and Holy Spirit.[112]

[107] Roman Catholic order for a funeral (adapted)

[108] Saint Augustine

[109] Adapted from John Baillie, 1949

[110] Gertrude of Thuringen, 1256-c.1303

[111] Carol Carretto, Letters from the Desert

[112] Louis Lambillotte (19th Century)

Gospel Reading: Luke 13:1-9

Just at that time some people came who told Jesus about the Galileans whose blood Pilate, the governor, had mixed with their sacrifices. ²Jesus replied to them, "Do you think that these Galileans were worse sinners than all *other* Galileans because they have suffered in this way? ³I tell you, no; but unless you change your old way of thinking, turn from your sinful ways and live changed lives, you will all likewise perish. ⁴Or do you assume that those eighteen on whom the tower in Siloam fell and killed were worse sinners than all the others who live in Jerusalem? ⁵I tell you, no; but unless you repent, you will all likewise perish." ⁶Then He *began* telling them this parable: "A certain man had a fig tree that had been planted in his vineyard; and he came looking for fruit on it, but did not find any; ⁷so he said to the vineyard-keeper, 'For three years I have come looking for fruit on this fig tree and have found none. Cut it down! Why does it even use up the ground, depleting the soil and blocking the sunlight?' ⁸But he replied to him, 'Let it alone, sir, just one more year until I dig around it and put in fertilizer; ⁹and if it bears fruit after this, fine; but if not, cut it down.

 (10)

Lord God have mercy on me. Jesus Christ, Son of God have mercy on me, a sinner. Lord I thank You for Your forgiveness and for the fact of Your sacrifice. Your shed blood makes me clean. You have said *but unless you repent, you too will perish*. So I do just that: I ask for the gift of repentance and I turn from my wicked ways. I do a 180 degree turn from following the devices and desires of my own heart. I turn to You, to Your ways, to Your means and to You as my Source and my God. I thank You that You have charged to my account the atoning act of Jesus Christ, the now Risen One, and You have clothed me with His righteousness. Fill me afresh this evening Holy Spirit that I might walk worthily. I thank You for Your patience and for Your second chances. I praise You for Your mercy.

O Merciful Father, You look upon the weaknesses of Your human children more in pity than in anger, and more in love than in pity. Let me now in Your holy presence inquire into the secrets of my heart. Have I today done anything to fulfill the purpose for which You caused me to be born? Have I accepted such opportunities of service as You in Your wisdom had set before my feet? Have I performed without omission the plain duties of the day? Give me grace to answer these questions honestly, O God. Have I today done anything to tarnish my Christian ideal of personhood? Have I been lazy in body or languid in spirit? Have I wrongfully indulged my bodily appetites? Have I kept my imagination pure and healthy? Have I been scrupulously honourable in all my work and business dealings? Have I been transparently sincere in all I have professed to be, to feel, or to do? Give me grace to answer honestly, O God. Have I tried today to see myself as others see me? Have I made more excuses for myself than I have been willing to make for others? Have I, in my own home, been a peace-maker or have I stirred up strife? Have I, while professing noble sentiments for great causes and distant objects, failed even in common charity and courtesy towards those nearest to me? Give me grace to answer honestly, O God. O Lord God whose infinite love, was made manifest in Jesus Christ and who, alone, has the power to destroy the empire of evil in my soul, grant that with each day that passes I may more and more be delivered from my besetting sins. Amen.[113]

O Holy Spirit, grant me the faith that will protect me from despair: deliver me from the lust of the flesh. Pour into my heart such love for You and for all persons that hatred and bitterness may be blotted out. Grant me the hope that will deliver me from fear and timidity. O Holy and Merciful God, Creator and Redeemer, Judge and Saviour, You know me and all that I do. You hate and punish evil without respect of persons. Please forgive the sins of those who heartily pray for forgiveness. You love goodness and reward it with a clear conscience, and in the world to come with a crown of righteousness.[114] Pardon, O Lord, my offences, voluntarily or involuntarily, wittingly or unwittingly committed, by word or deed, or in thought: forgive me those sins that are hidden, and those that are manifest; those that were done long ago, those which are known, and those which are forgotten but are known to You. Forgive me, O God, through Jesus Christ my Lord. Amen.[115]

Jesus, fill me with Your love now. I ask You to accept me and use me a little for Your glory. O God, I ask You, accept me and my service, and take all the glory for Yourself.[116]

---

[113] Adapted from John Baillie, 1949

[114] Dietrich Bonhoeffer

[115] Liturgy of Syrian of Jocobites

[116] David Livingstone, 1813-73

O God, who has bound me together in this bundle of life, give me grace to understand how my life depends on the industry, the honesty and integrity of my fellow pilgrims; that I may be mindful of their needs, grateful for their faithfulness, and faithful in my responsibilities to them, through Jesus Christ my Lord.[117] Use me, then, my Saviour, for whatever purpose, and in whatever way, You may require. Here is my poor heart, an empty vessel; fill it with Your grace. Here is my sinful and troubled soul; cleanse it, enliven it and refresh it with Your love. Take my heart for Your home; my mouth to spread abroad the glory of Your Name. At all times I may be enabled from the heart to say, Jesus needs me, and I am His.[118]

---

[117] Reinhold Niebuhr, 1892-1971

[118] Dwight L. Moody, 1837-99

Gospel Reading: Luke 13:10-21

Now Jesus was teaching in one of the synagogues on the Sabbath. [11]And there was a woman who for eighteen years had had an illness caused by a demon. She was bent double, and could not straighten up at all. [12]When Jesus saw her, He called her over and said to her, "Woman, you are released from your illness." [13]Then He laid His hands on her; and immediately she stood erect again and she *began* glorifying *and* praising God. [14]But the leader of the synagogue, indignant because Jesus had healed on the Sabbath, *began* saying to the crowd in response, "There are six days in which work ought to be done; so come on those days and be healed, and not on the Sabbath day." [15]But the Lord replied to him, "You play-actors and pretenders! Does not each one of you on the Sabbath untie his ox or his donkey from the stall and lead it away to water it? [16]And this woman, a descendant of Abraham whom Satan has bound for eighteen long years, should she not have been released from this bond on the Sabbath day?" [17]As He was saying this, all His opponents were being humiliated; and the entire crowd was rejoicing over all the glorious things that were being done by Him. [18]So this led Him to say, "What is the kingdom of God like? And to what shall I compare it? [19]It is like a mustard seed, which a man took and planted in his own garden; and it grew and became a tree, and the birds of the sky found shelter and nested in its branches." [20]And again He said, "To what shall I compare the kingdom of God? [21]It is like leaven, which a woman took and hid in three peck measures of flour until it was all leavened.

 (11)

Lord I am bent over with burdens I was not meant to bear on my own. I share these with You tonight. Thank You that You care for me 24/7. I realize that sometimes, as the pressure comes from life and work, I tend to bow my head to the ground and become more independent and less conscious of my deep need for You; for You to become my Sabbath, my Rest, and my Burden-bearer. May my faith grow like the mustard seed and expand as yeast. Your kingdom come on earth as it is in heaven today, O Lord.

The heavens declare Your glory and the the sky displays Your handiwork. You have given me the power to behold the beauty of Your world robed in all its splendor. The sun and the stars, the valleys and the hills, the rivers and the lakes each and all disclose Your presence. The roaring breakers of the sea tell of Your awesome might, the animals of the fields and forests and the birds of the air speak of Your wondrous will. In Your goodness You have made me able to hear the music of the world. Your divine voice sings through all creation.[119]

Almighty and ever-blessed God, You have left a witness with humankind, in every age. You have raised up saintly and prophetic people to lead the way of faith and love. I praise Your name for Saint Paul who said, *let all bitterness, and wrath, and anger, and clamour, and evil speaking, be put away from you, with all malice: and be kind to one another, tender-hearted, forgiving one another, even as God for Christ's sake has forgiven you.* O God, incline my heart to follow in this way. It was Saint Paul who said, *put on the Lord Jesus Christ, and make not provision for the flesh, to fulfil the lusts thereof.* O God, incline my heart to follow in this way. Saint Paul said, *let nothing be done through strife or pride; but in lowliness of mind let each esteem others better than themselves.* O God, incline my heart to follow in this way.

Saint Paul said, *he who glories, let him glory in the Lord.* O God, incline my heart to follow in this way. Saint Paul said, *continue in prayer, and watch with thanksgiving. Praying that God will open for us a door to speak the mystery of Christ.* O God, I pray tonight especially for all who, following in the footsteps of Saint Paul, are now labouring to bring the light of Christ's Gospel to this country and to the precious people in foreign lands. Amen.[120]

Dear Jesus, help me to spread Your fragrance everywhere I go. Penetrate and possess my whole being so utterly that my life may only be a radiance of Yours. Shine through me, and be so in me, that every person I come in contact with may feel Your presence. Let them look up and no longer see me but only Jesus! Let me preach You: by my example, by the sympathetic influence of what I do, and by the evident fullness of the love my heart bears for and from You.[121]

Deliver me, O God, from a slothful mind, from all lukewarmness, and all dejection of spirit. I know these deaden my love for You. Give me a lively, zealous, active, and cheerful spirit that I may vigorously perform whatever You command and

[120] Adapted from John Baillie, 1949

[121] Cardinal Newman, 1801-90 (Prayed daily by Mother Teresa's Missionaries of Charity)

[119] Traditional Jewish Prayer

thankfully suffer whatever You choose for me as I obey You in all things.[122]

O Lord, let Your peace rule in my heart. May Your strength be my song. I commit myself to Your care and keeping this night. Let Your grace be mighty in me, and let this grace work in me both to will and to do of Your own good pleasure. Grant me strength for all the duties of the upcoming day. May I live with others in peace and holy love, and grant that I follow Your every command with gladness. Give me grace to deny myself; to take up my cross daily, and to follow in the steps of my Lord and Master, Jesus Christ. Amen.[123]

There is a river whose streams make glad the city of God, the holy place where the Most High dwells. God is within her, she will not fall; God will help her at break of day. Nations are in an uproar, kingdoms fall; He lifts His voice, the earth meets. The LORD Almighty is with me; the God of Jacob is my fortress. Selah [pause].[124]

---

[122] John Wesley, 1703-91

[123] Matthew Henry

[124] Psalm 46:4-7

Gospel Reading: Luke 13:22-35

Jesus journeyed on through cities and villages, teaching and making His way toward Jerusalem. ²³And someone asked Him, "Lord, will only a few be saved from the penalties of the last judgment?" And He said to them, ²⁴"Strive to enter through the narrow door; for many, I tell you, will try to enter by their own works and will not be able. ²⁵Once the head of the house gets up and closes the door, and you begin to stand outside and knock on the door again and again, saying, 'Lord, open to us!' then He will answer you, 'I do not know where you are from for you are not of My household.' ²⁶Then you will begin to say, 'We ate and drank in Your presence, and You taught in our streets'; ²⁷but He will say to you, 'I do not know where you are from; depart from Me, all you evildoers!' ²⁸In that place there will be weeping in sorrow and pain and grinding of teeth in distress and anger when you see Abraham and Isaac and Jacob and all the prophets in the kingdom of God, but yourselves being thrown out *and* driven away. ²⁹And *people* will come from east and west, and from north and south, and they will sit down and feast at the table in the kingdom of God. ³⁰And behold, *some* are last who will be first, and *some* are first who will be last." ³¹At that very hour some Pharisees came up and said to Him, "Leave and go away from here, because Herod Antipas wants to kill You." ³²And He said to them, "Go and tell that fox, that sly, cowardly man, 'Listen carefully: I cast out demons and perform healings today and tomorrow, and on the third *day* I reach My goal.' ³³Nevertheless I must travel on today and tomorrow and the *day* after that—for it cannot be that a prophet would die outside of Jerusalem. ³⁴O Jerusalem, Jerusalem, who kills the prophets and stones to death those messengers who are sent to her by God! How often I have wanted to gather your children together around Me, just as a hen *gathers* her young under her wings, but you were not willing! ³⁵Listen carefully: your house is left to you desolate, abandoned by God and destitute of His protection; and I say to you, you will not see Me until *the time* comes when you say, 'Blessed is He who comes in the name of the Lord!'

☐ ☐ ☐ ☐ ☐ ☐ ☐ ☐ (12)

Blessed are You Lord Jesus, Messiah, the Annointed One. I give You thanks for Your steadfast and suffering journey to the Cross, to Your last breath, to death, then Your bodily resurrection from the dead. I thank You that You stand ready at the door and as I hear Your voice and open the door You promise to enter and accompany me. May I overcome as You over came. And may I be with You forever in glory.[125] Lord You have said *make every effort to enter through the narrow door*, help me to do so and to take my place, with those I love, at the feast of the kingdom of God. I choose this night to deny myself, to take up the cross and follow You. So help me Lord Jesus.

I thank You my God that, as a loving Father, those You love You rebuke and discipline. I thank You for Your call to me to be earnest and to repent.[126] Father in Heaven, You know every secret of my heart, all that I fear, all that I hope, and all of which I am ashamed. In this moment of confession, as I look into my heart and mind, have mercy upon me, and make me clean inside, that in all I do during this week I may behave justly and honestly. Let my motives be above suspicion. Let my word be my bond. Let me be slow to judge, knowing that I myself must one day be judged. I pray that Your Spirit would refill me, through Jesus Christ our Lord, Amen.[127]

You who are over me; You who are within me, may all see You in me. May I prepare the way for You, may I thank You for all that will fall to me this week. May I not forget the needs of others. Please keep me in Your love. May everything in my being be directed to Your glory and may I never despair. For I am under Your hand, and in You is all power and goodness. Give me a pure heart - that I may see You, a humble heart - that I may hear You, a heart of love - that I may serve You, a heart of faith - that I may abide in You. In Your hands, every moment has its meaning, its greatness, its glory, its peace and its coherence.[128]

Lord of my heart, give me vision to inspire me, that, working or resting, I may always think of You. Lord of my heart, give me light to guide me, that, at home or abroad, I may always walk in Your way. Lord of my heart, give me wisdom to direct me, that, thinking or acting, I may always discern right from wrong. Lord of my heart, give me courage to strengthen me, that, amongst friends or enemies, I may always proclaim Your justice. Lord of my heart, give me trust to console me, that, hungry or well-fed, I may always rely on Your mercy. Lord of my heart, save me from empty

[125] Revelations 3:20, 21

[126] Revelations 3:19

[127] Adapted from Peter Marshall (1902–67)

[128] Dag Hammarskjold

praise, that I may always boast of You. Lord of my heart, save me from power prowess, that I may always seek Your protection. Lord of my heart, save me from useless knowledge, that I may always study Your Word. Heart of my own heart, whatever befall me, rule over my thoughts and feelings, my words and action.[129]

Holy Father, thank You for helping me to understand that I can praise You as much in the ordinary affairs of life as in the unusual and more exciting things. Thank You that through the Lord Jesus, and through Him alone, I can continually offer to You a sacrifice of praise. I want to praise You by my attitudes as well as by my words and my actions. In the light of Your mercy to me, I want to do everything for You Lord Jesus. I commit myself now, with Your Spirit's help, to greater thankfulness, more wholehearted work, greater diligence in pursuing holiness.[130]

Come and see the works of the LORD, the desolations He has brought on the earth. He makes wars cease to the ends of the earth. He breaks the bow and shatters the spear. He burns the shields and chariots with fire. You say: *Be still and know that I am God; I will be exalted among the Nations, I will be exalted in the earth.* LORD Almighty You are with me; the God of Jacob is my fortress. Selah [pause].[131]

---

[129] Source unknown

[130] Derek Prime

[131] Psalm 46:8-11

Gospel Reading: Luke 14:1-11

It happened one Sabbath, when He went for a meal at the house of one of the ruling Pharisees, that they were watching Him closely *and* carefully hoping to entrap Him. [2]And there in front of Him was a man who had extreme swelling. [3]And Jesus asked the lawyers and the Pharisees, "Is it lawful to heal on the Sabbath, or not?" [4]But they kept silent. Then He took hold of the man and healed him, and sent him on his way. [5]Then He said to them, "Which one of you, having a son or an ox that falls into a well, will not immediately pull him out on the Sabbath day?" [6]And they were unable to reply to this. [7]Now Jesus *began* telling a parable to the invited guests when He noticed how they had been selecting the places of honor *at the table*, saying to them, [8]"When you are invited by someone to a wedding feast, do not sit down to eat at the place of honor, since a more distinguished person than you may have been invited by the host, [9]and he who invited both of you will come and say to you, 'Give this man your place,' and then, in disgrace you proceed to take the last place. [10]But when you are invited, go and sit down to eat at the last place, so that when your host comes, he will say to you, 'Friend, move up higher'; and then you will be honored in the presence of all who are at the table with you. [11]For everyone who exalts himself will be humbled before others, and he who *habitually* humbles himself and keeps a realistic self-view will be exalted.

 (13)

O Triune God, Father, Son and Spirit. I humble myself before Your holy presence. I come before You, not in my name but in the Name of the Lord Jesus Christ who invited me to do so. I come to Your throne, knowing of Your mercy and lovingkindness. I pray today for those in pain, those who suffer in body, soul and spirit. Lord, for those in anguish of loss, in anger, frustration, and disillusionment. For those who have been violated, abused, abandoned and dishonoured. For all of these I pray. Have mercy, restore, heal, reconcile and do justice I ask. I pray for Your grace in my life, in the lives of those close to me and in the lives of strangers. Move us all to a better place, intervene according to our various needs, through Jesus Christ who humbled Himself, even to the point of suffering the Cross for my sake.

How lovely is Your dwelling-place, O Lord of hosts! My soul desires and longs to enter the courts of the Lord. My heart sings joyfully to the living God. Happy are those who dwell in Your house; they will sing Your praises for ever.[132] O everlasting God, let the light of Your eternity fall upon my passing days. O holy God, let the light of Your perfect righteousness fall upon my sinful ways. O most merciful God, let the light of Your love pierce to the most secret corners of my heart and overcome the darkness of sin within me. Am I living as my conscience approves? Am I demanding of others a higher standard of conduct than I demand of myself? Am I taking a less charitable view of the failings of my neighbours than I am of my own? Am I standing in public for principles that I do not practise in private? Let my answer before You be truthful, O God. Do I ever allow bodily appetites to take precedence over spiritual interests? Do I ever allow the thought of my own gain to take precedence over the interests of the community? Am I, in my daily life, facing the stress of circumstance with courage and in dependence on You? Am I grateful for my many blessings? Am I allowing my happiness to be too dependent on money? On business, work and study success? Or on the good opinion of others? Is the sympathy I show to others who are in trouble commensurate with what I would expend on myself, if the same things happened to me? Let my answer before You be truthful, O God. Create in me a clean heart, O God; and renew a right spirit within me, through Jesus Christ. Amen.[133]

Dear Lord, help me keep my eyes on You. You are the incarnation of divine love. Jesus, You are the expression of God's infinite compassion. You are the visible manifestation of the Father's holiness. You are beauty, goodness, gentleness, forgiveness, and mercy. In You all can be found. Outside of You nothing can be found. Why should I look elsewhere or go elsewhere? You have the Words of eternal life. You are food and drink. You are the Way, the Truth, and the Life. You are the light that shines in the darkness, the lamp on the lampstand, and the house on the hilltop. O Holy One, Beautiful One, Glorious One, be my Lord, my Saviour, my Redeemer, my Guide, my Consoler, my Comforter, my Hope, my Joy, and my Peace. Let me be generous, not stingy or hesitant. Let me give You all - all I have, think, do,

[132] Psalm 84:1, 2, 4 Psalm 104:4

[133] Adapted from John Baillie, 1949

and feel. It is Yours, O Lord. Please accept it and make me fully Your own.[134]

O Christ of pure and perfect love, look on this sin-stained heart of mine! I want my life to be like Yours. Come and sanctify me now.[135] Almighty God, from whom no secrets are hid, cleanse the thoughts of my heart by the inspiration of Your Holy Spirit, that I may perfectly love You and worthily magnify Your holy Name, through Christ my Lord. Amen.[136]

I go to sleep tonight through a mighty strength: God's power to guide me, God's might to uphold me, God's eyes to watch over me, God's ear to hear me, God's Word to give me speech, God's hand to guard me, God's way to lie before me, God's shield to shelter me, and God's heavenly army to secure me.[137]

---

[134] Henri Nouwen

[135] William Booth

[136] Book of Common Prayer

[137] St. Bridgid of Gael (5th Century)

Gospel Reading: Luke 14:12-24

Jesus also went on to say to the one who had invited Him, "When you give a luncheon or a dinner, do not invite your friends or your brothers or your relatives or wealthy neighbors, otherwise they may also invite you in return and that will be your repayment. ^{13}But when you give a banquet *or* a reception, invite the poor, the disabled, the lame, and the blind, ^{14}and you will be blessed because they cannot repay you; for you will be repaid at the resurrection of the righteous." ^{15}When one of those who were reclining *at the table* with Him heard this, he said to Him, "Happy, prosperous, to be admired is he who will eat bread in the kingdom of God!" ^{16}But Jesus said to him, "A man was giving a big dinner, and he invited many *guests*; ^{17}and at the dinner hour he sent his servant to tell those who had been invited, 'Come, because everything is ready now.' ^{18}But they all alike began to make excuses. The first one said to him, 'I have purchased a piece of land and I have to go out and see it; please consider me excused.' ^{19}Another one said, 'I have purchased five yoke of oxen, and I am going to try them out; please consider me excused.' ^{20}And another said, 'I have recently married a wife, and for that reason I am unable to come.' ^{21}So the servant came back and reported this to his master. Then his master, the head of the household, became angry at the rejections of his invitation and said to his servant, 'Go out quickly into the streets and the lanes of the city and bring in here the poor and the disabled and the blind and the lame.' ^{22}And after returning, the servant said, 'Sir, what you commanded has been done, and still there is room.' ^{23}Then the master told the servant, 'Go out into the highways and along the hedges, and compel them to come in, so that my house may be filled with guests. ^{24}For I tell you, not one of those who were invited and declined will taste my dinner.'

☐ ☐ ☐ ☐ ☐ ☐ ☐ ☐ (14)

As the world's light fails, I seek the brightness of Your presence O Eternal Life. You know no weariness; now, as my limbs grow heavy and my spirit begins to flag, I commit myself to You. You never need sleep; now, as I lie down to sleep, I cast myself upon Your care. You keep watch when I lie helpless, I rely upon Your love.

Before I sleep, O God, I would review this day's doings in the light of Your eternity. I remember with sorrow the duties I have shirked. I remember with regret the hard words I have spoken. I remember with shame the unworthy thoughts I have harboured. Use these memories, O God, to help me to avoid the same tomorrow and then forever blot them out. I remember with gladness the beauty of the world today. I remember with sweetness the deeds of kindness I have seen done by others. I remember with thankfulness the work You enabled me to do and the truths You enabled me to learn. Use these memories, O God, to humble me, and let these live forever in my practice. For a moment, before I sleep, I rejoice in the friendships You have blessed my life with. And for all who tonight have nowhere to lay their heads or who, though lying down, cannot sleep for their pain or for their anxiety. For these I crave Your mercy and grace, in the Name of my Lord Christ. Amen.[138]

Lord Jesus, I give You my hands to do Your work. I give You my feet to go Your way. I give You my eyes to see as You see. I give You my tongue to speak Your Words. I give You my mind that You may think in me. I give You my spirit that You may pray in me. Above all, I give You my heart that You may love through me. I give You my whole self that You may grow in me. Lord Jesus, live, work and pray in me. I hand over to Your care, Lord, my soul and body, my prayers and my hopes, my health and my work, my life and my death, my parents, and my family, my friends and my neighbours, my country and all people with whom I have to do, today and always.[139]

I praise You Lord for Your sacrifice to create space for me in Your kingdom. I am grateful that through Jesus Christ I have a place with You forever. I thank You for my adoption into the family of God; for the eternal and transformative friendship offered to me with the Creator and Redeemer of the universe. Made in Your image and likeness I want to learn and practice hosting others, in ways that are authentic, need-meeting and honouring to You. May I be a person of hospitality and inclusion. Comfortable or not, may I open my heart and our home to those who are unable to reciprocate. Lord I am inclined to be an excuse maker. Separate me from this and help me to attend to the marginalized, to the disadvantaged and to help fill Your House with warmly honoured others.

---

[138] Adapted from John Baillie, 1949

[139] Adapted from Lancelot Andreives, 1555-1626

Lord, I do not know what to do with myself. So let me make this exchange: I will place myself entirely in Your hands, if You will cover my ugliness with Your beauty, and tame my unruliness with Your love. Put out the flames of false passion in my heart, since these flames destroy all that is true within me. Make me always live fully in Your service. Lord, I want no special signs from You, nor am I looking for intense emotions in response to Your love. I would rather be free of all emotion, than to run the danger of falling victim once again to false passion.[140]

Come, true Light. Come, Life Eternal. Come, Hidden Mystery. Come, Treasure without name. Come, Reality beyond all words. Come, Person beyond all understanding. Come, Rejoicing without end. Come, Light that knows no evening. Come, Unfailing Expectation of the saved. Come, Raising of the fallen. Come, Resurrection of the dead. Come, All Powerful, for unceasingly You create, refashion and change all things by Your will alone. Come, Invisible whom none may touch and handle. Come, for Your Name fills my heart with longing and is ever on my lips; yet who You are and what Your nature is, I cannot say or know. Come, Alone to the alone. Come, for You are Yourself the desire that is within me. Come, My Breath and My Life. Come, the Consolation of my humble soul. Come, My Joy, My Glory, My Endless Delight.[141]

---

[140] Catherine of Genoa, 1447-1510

[141] Saint Symeon the New Theologian

Gospel Reading: Luke 14:25-35

Now large crowds were going along with Jesus; and He turned and said to them, [26]"If anyone comes to Me, and does not hate his own father and mother and wife and children and brothers and sisters, yes, and even his own life in the sense of indifference to or relative disregard for them in comparison with his attitude toward God—he cannot be My disciple. [27]Whoever does not carry his own cross, expressing a willingness to endure whatever may come, and follow after Me with belief in Me, conforming to My example in living and, if need be, suffering or perhaps dying because of faith in Me, cannot be My disciple. [28]For which one of you, when he wants to build a watchtower for his guards, does not first sit down and calculate the cost, to see if he has enough to finish it? [29]Otherwise, when he has laid a foundation and is unable to finish the building, all who see it will begin to ridicule him, [30]saying, 'This man began to build and was not able to finish!' [31]Or what king, when he sets out to meet another king in battle, will not first sit down and consider whether he is strong enough with ten thousand men to encounter the one who is coming against him with twenty thousand? [32]Or else if he feels he is not powerful enough, while the other king is still a far distance away, he sends an envoy and asks for terms of peace. [33]So then, none of you can be My disciple who does not carefully consider the cost and then for My sake give up all his own possessions. [34]"Therefore, salt is good; but if salt has become tasteless, with what will it be seasoned? [35]It is fit neither for the soil nor for the manure pile; it is thrown away. He who has ears to hear, let him hear *and* heed My words.

 (15)

Lord Jesus I worship You above all; I give my life to You as a sincere act of devotion and dedication. You are my Lord and Master, there is no one before You. With all my heart, I want to be Your apprentice. Please be my guide and teacher; please superintend every corner of my life. Help me to understand what it means to carry my cross and follow You. Teach me to count the cost, pay the price and to lay the foundation required for You to continue to work Your perfect ways into my life. I set aside all I have, all I am, to be Your servant, Your disciple and Your instrument of reconciliation in the world. Refresh me, mold me, melt me, fill me and use me I pray.

Lord Jesus, You are the Way, the Truth, and the Life, hear me as I pray for the truth that shall make Your people free. Teach me that liberty is not only to be loved, but also to be lived. Liberty is too precious a thing to be buried in books. It cost too much to be hoarded. Make me to see that my liberty and the liberty of those who live in this country is not the right to do as one pleases, but the opportunity to be pleased to do what is right. So with this freedom may I do what is right; may Your blessing rest upon my labours; and may I have a good conscience, through Jesus Christ my Lord. Amen.[142]

I thank You for Pain, the sister of Joy. I thank You for Sorrow, the twin of Happiness. Pain, Joy, Sorrow, and Happiness are the four angels at work on the well of love. For the seasons of emotion in my heart, I thank You, O Lord.[143]

Oh Lord, I know not what to ask of You. You know my true needs. You love me more than I know how to love myself. I dare not ask for either a cross or consolation, I wait on You. My heart is open; visit and help me, for Your great mercy's sake. Strike me and heal me, cast me down and raise me up. I worship

Your holy will and inscrutable ways. I sacrifice myself to You and I put all my trust in You. To fulfil Your will, teach me how to pray.[144] Lord, where I am wrong make me willing to change, and where I am right make me easy to live with.[145] Lord, teach me patience while I am well. When I am sick either lighten my burden or strengthen my back. So often in my health I have presumed on my own strength.[146]

Receive me into Your protection, maintaining and increasing from day to day Your grace and goodness towards me, until You have brought me into the full and perfect unity of Your Son, Jesus Christ, my Lord; who is the true light of my soul. May it please You to forget all my sins past and by Your infinite mercy freely pardon me for each. Grant me these my petitions, O Father of mercy, for my Lord and Saviour, Jesus Christ's sake. Amen.[147]

Praise the Lord! The heavens adore You. Praise Him, angels, in the height; sun and moon, rejoice before Him; praise Him, all You stars and light. Praise the Lord! For You have spoken; worlds Your mighty voice have obeyed; laws which never shall

---

[142] Adapted from Peter Marshall (1902–67)
[143] Chandran Devanasen
[144] Source unknown
[145] Peter Marshall
[146] Thomas Fuller
[147] Liturgy of Geneva

be broken for their guidance You have made. Praise You Lord! For You are glorious; never shall Your promises fail; You, my God, have made Your saints victorious; sin and death shall not prevail. Praise You God of my salvation! The heavens on high, Your power proclaim; heaven and earth and all creation, laud and magnify Your Name.[148]

And You walk with me and You talk with me. And You tell me I am Your own. And the joy we share as we tarry here, none other has ever known. You speak to me and the sound of Your voice is so sweet that the birds hush their singing. And the melody that You give to me is within my heart now ringing. I will stay in the garden with You, though the night around me is falling. And the voice that I hear, falling on my ear, the Son of God discloses.[149] I bless You for Your willingness to have a loving and lasting relationship with me.

[148] Foundling Hospital Hymns, 1809

[149] Charles Austin Miles (1912)

Gospel Reading: Luke 15:1-10

Now all the tax collectors and sinners, including non-observant Jews, were coming near Jesus to listen to Him. [2]Both the Pharisees and the scribes *began* muttering *and* complaining, saying, "This man accepts *and* welcomes sinners and eats with them." [3]So He told them this parable: [4]"What man among you, if he has a hundred sheep and loses one of them, does not leave the ninety-nine in the wilderness and go after the one which is lost, searching until he finds it? [5]And when he has found it, he lays it on his shoulders, rejoicing. [6]And when he gets home, he calls together his friends and his neighbors, saying to them, 'Rejoice with me, because I have found my lost sheep!' [7]I tell you, in the same way there will be more joy in heaven over one sinner who repents than over ninety-nine righteous people who have no need of repentance. [8]"Or what woman, if she has ten silver coins, a day's wages, and loses one coin, does not light a lamp and sweep the house and search carefully until she finds it? [9]And when she has found it, she calls together her women friends and neighbors, saying, 'Rejoice with me, because I found the lost coin!' [10]In the same way, I tell you, there is joy in the presence of the angels of God over one sinner who repents. That is, a sinner who changes his or inner self—the old way of thinking, regrets past sins, lives their life in a way that proves repentance; and seeks God's purpose for their life.

 (16)

Dear Lord, I imagine You as so madly in love with Your creatures that You decided to live with us. You created me; and then, even though I had turned away from You, You redeemed me. You are God and have no need of me. Your greatness is made no greater by my creation; Your power is made no stronger by my redemption. You have no duty to care for me, no debt to repay me. It is love, and love alone, which has moved You.[150]

Thank You for Your seeking and saving work. I give you thanks for the gift of repentance and for the invitation to me to turn from the devices and desires of my own heart to follow in Your ways; to do an "about turn" and to follow You. I rejoice with You when the lost are found, when the repentant turns to You. Lord Jesus Christ You pursue with joy those You love. Here I am Lord, Your

---

[150] Catherine of Siena, 1347-80

servant, Your needy and lost sheep calls out to You. May I ever share Your joy as Your transformational work translates the dead to life and turns wicked sinners into righteous and forgiven children. I praise You for Your love and Your pursuit of me and those I love. I worship You for Your loving kindness and mercy, O Lord. I love You.

You are clearly most wise, most great, most holy, full of wisdom and power and tender mercy. You created me in Your own image. You have given me this life to live, You have set the bounds of my living and circumstance. You have surrounded me with gracious and beneficent influences. You have written Your law within my heart. And in my heart's most secret chamber You have waited to meet and speak with me, freely offering me Your fellowship in spite of all my sinning. I avail myself of this peace of mind and meeting with You O Lord. Let me approach Your presence humbly and reverently. Let me leave behind all fretfulness, all un-worthy desires, all thoughts of malice towards my fellow beings, and all hesitancy in surrendering my will to Yours. In Your will, O Lord, is my peace. In Your love is my rest. In Your service is my joy. You are all my heart's desire. Whom have I in heaven but You? No one! In Your presence,

O God, I think not only of myself, but of others, especially my family and friends. I think of those who today have worked or interacted with me, of those who are in sorrow, of those who are bearing the burdens of others, of those who have taken on difficult situations and those who are called to work in tragic situations for Your Kingdom sake. You are one God and Father, be near to us all tonight and graciously keep watch over our souls. Hear my prayer for Jesus Christ's sake. Amen.[151]

O God my Father, I thank You for all the bright things of life. Help me to see them, and to count them, and to remember them, that my life may flow in ceaseless praises, for the sake of Jesus Christ my Lord.[152] My God, I am not my own but Yours. Take me for Your own, and help me in all things to do Your holy will. My God, I give myself to You, in joy and sorrow, in sickness and in health, in success and in failure, in life and in death, in time and for eternity, make me and keep me Your own, through Jesus Christ my Lord.[153]

This, O Father, is life everlasting, to know You, the only True God, and Jesus Christ whom You sent. And so, I

---

[151] Adapted from John Baillie, 1949

[152] J. H. Jowett, 1846-1923

[153] Source unknown

pray to You, increase my faith, that this knowledge may evermore dwell in me. Increase my obedience, that I may not swerve from Your commandments, and increase my firm hold of You. Multiply Your grace upon me, that being daily more dead to sin and alive to You, I may be constantly led by Your Holy Spirit: fearing You only. You are most worthy to be feared and reverently obeyed. I glory in You only, You are the glory of all Your saints. I desire nothing but You. You are of all the worthiest and the best. May I, at the last, live and dwell with You forever.[154]

I am weak, but You are strong; Jesus, keep me from all wrong. I'll be satisfied as long as I walk, let me walk close to You. Just a closer walk with Thee, grant it, Jesus, is my plea. Daily walking close to Thee, let it be, dear Lord, let it be.[155]

---

[154] Desiderius Erasmus

[155] Author unknown

Gospel Reading: Luke 15:11-32

Then He said, "A certain man had two sons. ¹²The younger of them inappropriately said to his father, 'Father, give me the share of the property that falls to me.' So he divided the estate between them. ¹³A few days later, the younger son gathered together everything that he had and traveled to a distant country, and there he wasted his fortune in reckless *and* immoral living. ¹⁴Now when he had spent everything, a severe famine occurred in that country, and he began to do without *and* be in need. ¹⁵So he went and forced himself on one of the citizens of that country, who sent him into his fields to feed pigs. ¹⁶He would have gladly eaten the carob pods that the pigs were eating but they could not satisfy his hunger, and no one was giving *anything* to him. ¹⁷But when he finally came to his senses, he said, 'How many of my father's hired men have more than enough food, while I am dying here of hunger! ¹⁸I will get up and go to my father, and I will say to him, "Father, I have sinned against heaven and in your sight. ¹⁹I am no longer worthy to be called your son; just treat me like one of your hired men."' ²⁰So he got up and came to his father. But while he was still a long way off, his father saw him and was moved with compassion *for him*, and ran and embraced him and kissed him. ²¹And the son said to him, 'Father, I have sinned against heaven and in your sight; I am no longer worthy to be called your son.' ²²But the father said to his servants, 'Quickly bring out the best robe for the guest of honor and put it on him; and give him a ring for his hand, and sandals for his feet. ²³And bring the fattened calf and slaughter it, and let us invite everyone to feast and celebrate; ²⁴for this son of mine was as good as dead and is alive again; he was lost and has been found.' So they began to celebrate. ²⁵"Now his older son was in the field; and when he returned and approached the house, he heard music and dancing. ²⁶So he summoned one of the servants and *began* asking what this celebration meant. ²⁷And he said to him, 'Your brother has come, and your father has killed the fattened calf because he has received him back safe and sound.' ²⁸But the elder brother became angry *and* deeply resentful and was not willing to go in; and his father came out and *began* pleading with him. ²⁹But he said to his father, 'Look! These many years I have served you, and I have never neglected *or* disobeyed your command. Yet you have never given me so much as a young goat, so that I might celebrate with my friends; [30] but when this other son of yours arrived, who has devoured your estate with immoral women, you slaughtered that fattened calf for him!' [31]The father said to him, 'Son, you are always with me, and all that is mine is yours. [32]But it was fitting to celebrate and rejoice, for this brother of yours was as good as dead and *has begun* to live. He was lost and has been found.'

 (17)

I praise You for the life that stirs within me. I praise You for the bright and beautiful world into which I go. I praise You for earth and sea and sky, for clouds and singing birds. I praise You for the work You have given me to do. I praise You for all that You have given me to fill my leisure hours. I praise You for my family and friends. I praise You for music, books, good company, good places to be and for all pure pleasures.[156]

Lord I give You thanks that You have an unquenchable love for returning prodigals. Tonight I admit that I have sinned against heaven and You. You celebrate the lost being found. May I join in Your delight and celebration as other members of Your family come home to their God and as they are received with the love of their Father in heaven. Today I thank You for earthy parents and for sibblings who, at their best, love and support. You have placed the solitary in families. For those who are distant

and those who know the ravages of dysfunction, benefit these with Your presence, Your warm embrace and secure accompaniment in life. Thank You for the impulse, insight, and sensibility that graces those who return home to where they belong and for their acceptance, through Jesus Christ.

O Lord You have the Words of eternal life. Help me to cultivate proper speech. Surrounded as I am with noble inscriptions and writings of the plain, stirring words of wise men and women. Lord, may I say what I mean and mean what I say; and may what I say be worth saying. Teach me economy in speech that neither wounds nor offends, that affords light without unnecessarily generating heat. Bridle my tongue lest my words create a stampede of utterances for which I will be ashamed. O Lord God, in the midst of troubles that surround the world and those I love, when compromises come home to roost and expediencies return to plague me, please keep me from adding to the

[156] John Baillie, 1886-1960

mistakes of the past. Save me from accepting a little of what I know to be wrong in order to get a little of what I imagine to be right. Help me to stand up with courage for the inalienable rights and responsibilities of humankind and the just principles, knowing that Your power and Your blessing will be upon all of us only when we are in the right and do what is good and virtuous. May I so speak and live, as to merit Your blessing, through Jesus Christ my Lord.[157]

O Lord my God, You are above all the best, the strongest and the most high. You alone are most full and most sufficient; You alone are the sweetest, full of consolation. You alone are the most noble and glorious, for in You are gathered all good things. Never will my heart find rest unless it rests with You. You are the brightness of eternal glory. You are the comfort of the pilgrim soul. With You is my tongue without voice, and my very silence speaks to You. Come, oh come, for without You I shall have no joyful day or hour; for You are my joy, and without You my table is empty. Praise and glory be to You. Let my mouth, my soul, and all creatures together, praise and bless You.[158]

O God, what a fool I am to live with a grudge when I can live with grace. If there are any grudges in my heart then I ask you to uproot them now. Cleanse me from every sin, I ask in Jesus' Name. I don't want to stumble around in the darkness, make myself and those I live with miserable. Help me to remove every trace of bitterness and hatred from my heart this night and may I walk in the light - the light of Your love. Search my heart to see if there is any wicked way in me. I want to rise, from this moment, to a life of wholeness and obedience. Help me, dear Lord. Heavenly Father, help me. Make generosity the basis of all my dealings with everyone I meet. And not just tomorrow but every day. Help me be the channel, not the stopping place, of Your generosity. In Christ's name I ask it.[159]

The heavens declare Your glory, Lord. In every star Your wisdom shines; but when my eyes behold Your Word, I read Your Name in fairer lines. Your blest wonders here I view in souls renewed, and sins forgiven. Lord cleanse my sins, my soul renew, and make Your Word my guide to heaven.[160]

---

[157] Adapted from Peter Marshall (1902–67)
[158] Thomas a Kempis, c.1380-1471
[159] Selwyn Hughes
[160] Isaac Watts (1674-1748)

Gospel Reading: Luke 16:1-18

Now Jesus was also saying to the disciples, "There was a certain rich man who had a manager of his estate, and accusations against this man were brought to him, that this man was squandering his master's possessions. ²So he called him and said to him, 'What is this I hear about you? Give an accounting of your management of my affairs, for you can no longer be my manager.' ³The manager of the estate said to himself, 'What will I do, since my master is taking the management away from me? I am not strong enough to dig for a living, and I am ashamed to beg. ⁴I know what I will do, so that when I am removed from the management, people who are my master's debtors will welcome me into their homes.' ⁵So he summoned his master's debtors one by one, and he said to the first, 'How much do you owe my master?' ⁶He said, 'A hundred measures of olive oil.' And he said to him, 'Take your bill, and sit down quickly and write fifty.' ⁷Then he said to another, 'And how much do you owe?' He said, 'A hundred measures of wheat.' He said to him, 'Take your bill, and write eighty.' ⁸And his master commended the unjust manager not for his misdeeds, but because he had acted shrewdly by preparing for his future unemployment; for the sons of this age the non-believers are shrewder in relation to their own kind that is, to the ways of the secular world than are the sons of light the believers. ⁹And I tell you learn from this, make friends for yourselves for eternity by means of the wealth of unrighteousness that is, use material resources as a way to further the work of God, so that when it runs out, they will welcome you into the eternal dwellings. ¹⁰"He who is faithful in a very little thing is also faithful in much; and he who is dishonest in a very little thing is also dishonest in much. ¹¹Therefore if you have not been faithful in the *use of* earthly wealth, who will entrust the true *riches* to you? ¹²And if you have not been faithful in *the use of* that earthly wealth which belongs to another whether God or man, and of which you are a trustee, who will give you that which is your own? ¹³No servant can serve two masters; for either he will hate the one and love the other, or he will stand devotedly by the one and despise the other. You cannot serve *both* God and mammon that is, your earthly possessions or anything else you trust in and rely on instead of God."

¹⁴Now the Pharisees, who were lovers of money, were listening to all these things and were sneering *and* ridiculing Him. ¹⁵So He said to them, "You are the ones who declare yourselves just *and* upright in the sight of men, but God knows your hearts, your thoughts, your desires, and your secrets; for that which is highly esteemed among men is detestable in the sight of God. ¹⁶"The Law and the writings of the Prophets were proclaimed until John; since then the gospel of the kingdom of God has been *and* continues to be preached, and everyone tries forcefully to go into it. ¹⁷Yet it is easier for heaven and earth to pass away than for a single stroke of a letter of the Law to fail *and* become void. ¹⁸"Whoever divorces his wife and marries another commits adultery, and he who marries one who is divorced from her husband commits adultery.

 (18)

Glory be to You, O Lord, glory to You, O holy One, glory to You, O King![161] *Worthy are You, our Lord and God, to receive glory, honour and blessing.*[162] O Lord my God, You have called Your servant to stand in Your house and to serve at Your altar. To You and to Your service I devote myself, body, soul, and spirit. Fill my memory with the record of Your mighty works; enlighten my understanding with the light of Your Holy Spirit; and may all the desires of my heart focus on what You would have me do.[163]

I praise You for the good news of the kingdom of God and that this Gospel is being preached throughout the world, touching the hearts of many. I am grateful for Your tansforming work in my life O God. You know my heart. I acknowledge that only one master can be properly served. You are my Master and Lord. To You I owe allegiance, loyalty and my very life. Tonight I dedicate myself to You and to Your service. You have given me much; may I be found to be trustworthy, honest and wise in all You have given me to steward. Lord help me in matters of money, transactions and in all the managing and leading interactions I have with others. Help me to build relationships of trust with others, by my integrity, respect and care for them. May my authenticity and true-faced living, with You as my Source, be the explanation for the favour I have with others. So help me to please You in all I do, all I give, and the way I live.

[161] John Chrysostom, c.347-407

[162] Revelation 4:10, 11; 5:8

[163] The Book of Common Prayer of the Episcopal Church, USA

O GOD, immortal, eternal, invisible, I remember with gladness and thanksgiving all that You are to this world. You are Companion to the brave, Upholder to the loyal, Light to the wanderer, Joy to the pilgrim, Guide to the pioneer, Helper to labouring persons, Refuge to the broken-hearted, Deliverer to the oppressed, Advocate to the tempted, Strength to the victorious, Leader to rulers, Friend to the poor, Rescuer to the perishing, and Hope to the dying. Give me faith now to believe that You are all in all to me, according to my need; if only I renounce all proud self-dependence and put my trust in You. The difficulty of living well should remind me to not fall into any kind of heedlessness or despair. Show Your lovingkindness tonight, O Lord, to all who stand in need of Your help. Be with the weak to make them strong and with the strong to make them gentle. Cheer the lonely with Your company and the distracted with Your solitude. Prosper Your Church in the fulfillment of Her mighty task, and grant Your blessing to all who have toiled today in Christ's name. Amen.[164]

God, I give You praise for a day well spent. But I am yet unsatisfied, because I do not enjoy enough of You. I want my soul to be more closely united to You. You know Lord that I love You above all things. You made me, You know my desires, and my expectations. It is Your favour, Your acceptance, and the communications of Your grace that I earnestly wish for more than anything in the world. I rejoice that You are my Father, my Lord and my God. I thank You that You have brought me so far.[165] Grant that I may never presume on my own might and power; but, I acknowledge my own infirmity, frailty, and weakness. May I receive at Your mighty hand strength to perform Your holy and blessed will.[166]

God, You are in favour of revival. Other needs are insignificance compared to the need for a *deep and* widespread revival. A revival that fills the hearts of saints with holy love and so burdens the hearts of God's ministers that the Word of God is like fire shut up in their bones. A revival that makes both the Church and the world *realise the* shortness of time and the importance of eternity. A revival that is so much of heaven and so much of God's glory that all the world will be compelled to see and feel Your mighty influence.[167]

---

[164] Adapted from John Baillie, 1949

[165] Susanna Wesley, 1669-1742

[166] Thomas Cramner

[167] A Prayer for Revivial (Part One) (An excerpt from a prayer published in 1904 in Old Time Religion Magazine)

Light of the world! Forever, ever shining, there is no change in You; True Light of life, all joy and health enshrining, You cannot fade nor flee. Light of the world! Undimming and unsetting, O shine each mist away; banish the fear, the falsehood, and the fretting; be my unchanging Day.[168] Renew my love for You my God. Fill me with Yourself.

[168] Horatius Bonar (1808-1889)

Gospel Reading: Luke 16:19-31

Now there was a certain rich man who was habitually dressed in expensive purple and fine linen, and celebrated *and* lived joyously in splendor every day. ²⁰And a poor man named Lazarus, was laid at his gate, covered with sores. ²¹He eagerly longed to eat the *crumbs* which fell from the rich man's table. Besides, even the dogs were coming and licking his sores. ²²Now it happened that the poor man died and his spirit was carried away by the angels to Abraham's bosom, paradise; and the rich man also died and was buried. ²³In Hades, the realm of the dead, being in torment, he looked up and saw Abraham far away and Lazarus in his bosom. ²⁴And he cried out, 'Father Abraham, have mercy on me, and send Lazarus so that he may dip the tip of his finger in water and cool my tongue, because I am in severe agony in this flame.' ²⁵But Abraham said, 'Son, remember that in your lifetime you received your good things, and Lazarus likewise bad things; but now he is comforted here in paradise, while you are in severe agony. ²⁶And besides all this, between us and you people a great chasm has been fixed, so that those who want to come over from here to you will not be able, and none may cross over from there to us.' ²⁷So the rich man said, 'Then, father Abraham, I beg you to send Lazarus to my father's house— ²⁸for I have five brothers—in order that he may *solemnly* warn them *and* witness to them, so that they too will not come to this place of torment.' ²⁹But Abraham said, 'They have the Scriptures given by Moses and the writings of the Prophets; let them listen to them.' ³⁰He replied, 'No, father Abraham, but if someone from the dead goes to them, they will repent.' ³¹And he said to him, 'If they do not listen to the messages of Moses and the Prophets, they will not be persuaded even if someone rises from the dead.'

 (19)

I want to listen and learn Lord. By Your Holy Spirit, my conscience, Your Word and my senses teach me what I need to know and incorporate into my thinking and feelings. Thank You for Moses, the prophets, the apostles and saints. Open my heart to Your teaching – help me to have the humility of heart to follow You. In my lifetime I have received much good – help me to provide for those with less – may I be generous even as You have been generous to me. I recall the grace of the Lord Jesus

Christ, who though He was rich for my sake He became poor, so that through His poverty I might become rich.[169]

Lord God of Hosts, You are intimately concerned for well over seven billion human creatures all over the earth, and yet You are just as concerned about me as if I were an only child. You understand how hard it is to work and live with the clamour of voices in my ears. Amid all the din of voices, give me the willingness to take time to listen to Your voice. I know that if I follow the still small voice within, all those You've entrusted to me will be served fairly, and all will get what they deserve from my service. Father in heaven, as I pray for Your guidance and help, I know that You do not intend prayer to be a substitute for work. I know that I am expected to do my part, for You have not made me a puppet, but a person with mind to think and a will to resolve. Make me willing to think, and think hard, clearly, and honestly; guided by Your voice within me, and the light You have given. May I never fail to do the very best I can. In anticipation of tomorrow help me to rest now to work in the morning as if it all depended on me, that I may do that which is well pleasing in Your

sight and be doing so in absolute dependence on You, for Jesus' sake. Amen.[170]

Lord Jesus, You experienced, in person, torture and death as a prisoner of conscience. You were beaten and flogged and sentenced to an agonizing death though You had done no wrong. Be now with prisoners of conscience throughout the world. Be with them in their fear and loneliness, in the agony of physical and mental torture, and in the face of execution and death. Stretch out Your hands in power to break their chains. Be merciful to the oppressor and the torturer and place a new heart within them. Forgive all injustice in our lives and transform us to be instruments of Your peace, for by Your wounds we are healed.[171]

Make me worthy, Lord, to serve my fellow human beings throughout the world who live and die in poverty and hunger. Give them, through my hands, this day their daily bread, and through my understanding of their needs, give them love, peace and joy.[172]

I thank You for the mercies of the past month. I have laid down and slept at night, and each morning I have awakened again and again in safety. Because You have sustained me, I am

---

[169] 2 Corinthians 8:9

[170] Adapted from Peter Marshall (1902–67)

[171] Amnesty International

[172] (Mother) Teresa of Calcutta

brought safety to the beginning of one day after another. I acknowledge that often I have been cold and defective in my love for You. I am weak in my desires after You and do not walk with You as I ought to. But I pray that You will forgive all my sins for Christ's sake, and be at peace with me. Grant me strength for all the duties of the day; that I may do all things such that You are acknowledged in all my ways.[173]

O Lord, let me not desire health or life, except to spend them for You, with You, and in You. You alone know what is good for me. Do, therefore, what seems best to You. Give to me, or take from me; conform my will to Yours; and grant that, with humble and perfect submission, and in holy confidence, I may receive the orders of Your eternal Providence; and may equally adore all that comes to me from You, through Jesus Christ my Lord. Amen.[174]

---

[173] Matthew Henry

[174] Blaise Pascal

Gospel Reading: Luke 17:1-19

Jesus said to His disciples, "Stumbling blocks, temptations and traps set to lure one to sin are sure to come, but judgment is coming to him through whom they come! [2]It would be better for him if a millstone as large as one turned by a donkey were hung around his neck and he were hurled into the sea, than for him to cause one of these little ones to stumble in sin and lose faith. [3]Pay attention *and* always be on guard looking out for one another! If your brother sins *and* disregards God's precepts, solemnly warn him; and if he repents *and* changes, forgive him. [4]Even if he sins against you seven times a day, and returns to you seven times and says, 'I repent,' you must give up resentment and consider the offense recalled and annulled." [5]The apostles said to the Lord, "Increase our ability to confidently trust in God and in His power." [6]And the Lord said, "If you have confident, abiding faith in God even as small as a mustard seed, you could say to this mulberry tree which has very strong roots, 'Be pulled up by the roots and be planted in the sea'; and if the request was in agreement with the will of God it would have obeyed you. [7]"Which of you who has a servant plowing or tending sheep will say to him when he comes in from the field, 'Come at once and sit down to eat?' [8]Will he not instead say to him, 'Prepare something for me to eat, and *appropriately* clothe yourself for service and serve me while I eat and drink; then afterward you may eat and drink?' [9]He does not thank the servant just because he did what he was ordered to do, does he? [10]So you too, when you have done everything that was assigned *and* commanded you, say, 'We are unworthy servants undeserving of praise or a reward, for we have not gone beyond our obligation; we have *merely* done what we ought to do.'" [11]While Jesus was on the way to Jerusalem, He was passing along the border between Samaria and Galilee. [12]As He entered a village, He was met by ten lepers who stood at a distance; [13]and they raised their voices and called out, "Jesus, Master, have mercy on us!" [14]When He saw them, He said to them, "Go and show yourselves to the priests." And as they went, they were miraculously healed *and* made clean. [15]One of them, when he saw that he was healed, turned back, glorifying *and* praising *and* honoring God with a loud voice; [16]and he lay face downward at Jesus' feet, thanking Him over and over. He was a Samaritan. [17]Then Jesus asked, "Were not ten of you cleansed? Where are the other nine? [18]Was there no one found to return and to give thanks *and* praise to God, except this foreigner?" [19]Jesus said to him, "Get up and go on your way. Your personal trust in Me and your confidence in God's power has restored you to health.

 (20)

For grace to live so as not to harm or negatively influence others I pray. Instead, may I demonstrate by my life lived in dependence on You, what integrity and right living, doing good, and being virtuous are about. Help me to help others to live without sin, to live without enmity and to be a full participant in a life that forgives and has been fully forgiven. I say with the disciples: Please increase my faith and give me the wherewithal to obey Your commandments and to be a worthy servant. Jesus, Master, have pity on me, cleanse me, heal me and make me well. I praise You. May my life be a 24/7 expression of praise and worship. When I wake in the morning may I rise and go, refreshed, revived and ready to do Your good, perfect and pleasing will with delight and with the experience of having Your joy as my strength.

O Creator of all things, I lift up my heart in gratitude to You for this day's happiness. For the mere joy of living, for all the sights and sounds around me, for all things bright and beautiful, for friendship and good company, for work to perform and the skill and strength to perform it, for time to play when the day's work is done, and for health and a glad heart to enjoy it. O eternal Father, let me never think that I am here to stay. Let me still remember that I am a stranger and pilgrim on the earth. Preserve me by Your grace, good Lord, from so losing myself in the joys of earth that I have no longing left for the purer joys of heaven. May the happiness of this day not become a snare to my overly worldly heart. And if, instead of happiness, I have today suffered any disappointment or defeat, if there has been any sorrow where I had hoped for joy, or sickness where I had looked for health, give me grace to accept this experience as a loving reminder that this is not my home. I thank You, O Lord, that You have so set eternity within my heart that no earthly thing can ever completely satisfy me.[175]

Lord, I remember the millions in this world who must go hungry today, all those who do not have even the basic necessities of life, and for whom life itself has become a burden. Out of

_____

[175] Adapted from John Baillie, 1949

the depths I cry to You, Lord, hear my cry and listen to my prayer. Lord, remember all those who because of their caste or class, colour or sex are exploited and marginalized. Lord You know the forces of oppression that trample on people and the unjust systems which break the spirit of people, and rob them of their rights and dignity. Out of the depths I cry to You, Lord, hear my cry and listen to my prayer.[176]

Lord, I know I am getting older. Keep me from thinking I must say something on every subject, on every occasion. Take away my craving to straighten out everybody's affairs. Keep my mind free from the recital of endless details; give me wings to get to the point. Seal my lips on my aches and pains, despite their increasing frequency. I dare to ask for a growing humility and lessening cocksureness when my memory clashes with the memories of others. Teach me that occasionally I may be mistaken.[177]

Almighty God, Father, Son and Holy Spirit, I lift my heart in adoration to You this day. You are my Creator, my Redeemer, my Sanctifier, my Preserver, my Provider and my All in All. The great desire of my heart is to know You and to make You known.

Purify me from every sin and set my heart ablaze with love for You. Too often my prayers have become my sin because of their coldness. May I be satisfied with nothing less than turning the world upside down. Take the brief span of my life and use it for the advancement of the kingdom of Lord Jesus Christ. In Your most glorious Name I pray. Amen.[178]

[176] World Council of Churches

[177] Source unknown

[178] James Kennedy

Gospel Reading: Luke 17:20-37

Now having been asked by the Pharisees when the kingdom of God would come, He replied, "The kingdom of God is not coming with signs to be observed *or* with a visible display; [21]nor will people say, 'Look! Here it is!' or, 'There it is!' For the kingdom of God is among you because of My presence." [22]Then He said to the disciples, "The time will come when you will long to see even one of the days of the Son of Man, and you will not see it. [23]They will say to you, 'Look the Messiah is there!' *or* 'Look He is here!' Do not go away to see Him, and do not run after *them*. [24]For just like the lightning, when it flashes out of one part of the sky, gives light to the other part of the sky, so visible will the Son of Man be in His day. [25]But first He must suffer many things and be repudiated *and* rejected *and* considered unfit to be the Messiah by this unbelieving generation. [26]And just as it was in the days of Noah, so it will be in the time of the second coming of the Son of Man: [27]the people were eating, they were drinking, they were marrying, they were being given in marriage, they were indifferent to God until the day that Noah went into the ark, and the flood came and destroyed them all. [28]It was the same as it was in the days of Lot. People were eating, they were drinking, they were buying, they were selling, they were planting, they were building carrying on business as usual, without regard for their sins; [29]but on the very day that Lot left Sodom it rained fire and burning sulfur from heaven and destroyed them all. [30]It will be just the same on the day that the Son of Man is revealed. [31]On that day, whoever is on the housetop, with his belongings in the house, must not come down and go inside to take them out; and likewise whoever is in the field must not turn back. [32]Remember what happened to Lot's wife when she looked back! [33]Whoever seeks to save his life will eventually lose it through death, and whoever loses *his life* in this world will keep it from the consequences of sin and separation from God. [34]I tell you, on that night when Messiah comes again there will be two sleeping in one bed; the one the non-believer will be taken away in judgment and the other the believer will be left. [35]There will be two women grinding at the mill together; the one, the non-believer, will be taken away in judgment and the other, the believer, will be left. [36]Two men will be in the field; one will be taken and the

> other will be left." [37]And they asked Him, "Where, Lord?" He answered, "Where the corpse is, there the vultures will be gathered.

☐ ☐ ☐ ☐ ☐ ☐ ☐ ☐ (21)

God, above whom is nothing, beyond whom is nothing, without whom is nothing. God, under whom is the whole, in whom is the whole, with whom is the whole. Hear me, graciously hear me, my God, my Lord, my King, my Father, my Cause, my Hope, my Wealth, my Honour, my House, my Country, my Health, my Light, and my Life.[179]

Lord help me to be wise in my living. I realize that, a person is no fool who gives what cannot be kept (my life) to gain what cannot be lost (eternal life).[180] I pray that Your kingdom would come on earth as it is in heaven. Thank You for Your kingship over my life. I intend, with Your help, to seek first Your kingdom in all I do. Lord You alone give the kingdom of God,[181] appoint the kingdom,[182] declare for whom it shall be,[183] and issue the invitation.[184] I know I must become as a child and to pray for Your kingdom to come.[185] So

I watch and pray for Your kingdom to come on earth as it is in heaven.

God of love, whose compassion never fails; I bring before You the troubles and perils of people and Nations, the sighing of prisoners and captives, the sorrows of the bereaved, the necessities of strangers, the helplessness of the weak, the despondency of the weary, and the failing powers of the aged. O Lord, draw near to each of these, for the sake of Jesus Christ their Lord.[186]

O Heavenly Father, give me a heart like the heart of Jesus Christ, a heart more ready to minister than to be ministered unto, a heart moved by compassion towards the weak and the oppressed, a heart set upon the coming of Your kingdom. I pray tonight, O God, for all those sorts and conditions of persons to whom Jesus Christ was wont to give special thought and care. I pray for those lacking food or drink or clothing. I pray for the sick and all who are wasted by disease. Tonight I pray for the blind, for the maimed and lame, for lepers, for prisoners, and for those oppressed by any injustice. I pray for the lost sheep of our human

---

[179] Saint Augustine
[180] Jim Elliot
[181] Luke 12:52
[182] Luke 22:29f
[183] Matthew 5:3; Mark 10:14
[184] Luke 14:15-24
[185] Mark 10:15; Matthew 6:10

[186] Anselm. 1033-1109

society, for all fallen and exploited women and for all lonely strangers. For the worried and anxious, for those who are living faithful lives in obscurity, for those who are fighting bravely in unpopular causes, for all who are labouring diligently in Your vineyard. For these requests I pray.

Dear Father, make me the channel through which Your divine love may reach the hearts and lives of those who are nearest to me. Amen.[187] Grant, O Father, that Your lovingkindness in causing my own lines to fall in pleasant places may make me sensitive to the needs of others, more inclined to heartfelt intercession for them, placing their burdens on Your adoring shoulders. And if any adversity should befall me, then let me not brood upon my own sorrows, as if I alone were suffering, but rather let me busy myself in the compassionate service of all who need my help. Let the power of my Lord Christ be strong within me and His peace invade my spirit.[188]

My God, I am wholly Yours. God of Love, I love You with all my heart. Lord, fashion me according to Your heart.[189] I bind to me today the power of God to hold and lead, Your eye to watch, Your might to secure, and Your ear to pay attention to my need. Your wisdom, my God, to teach, Your hand to guide, Your shield to ward off dangers, the Word of God to give me speech, and Your heavenly army to be my guard. Christ be with me, Christ within me, Christ behind me, Christ before me, Christ beside me, Christ to win me, Christ to comfort and restore me, Christ beneath me, Christ above me, Christ in quiet, Christ in danger, Christ in mouth of friend and stranger, Christ in hearts of all who love me.[190]

---

[187] Adapted from John Baillie, 1949

[188] Adapted from John Baillie, 1949

[189] Brother Lawrence

[190] Saint Patrick (attributed)

Gospel Reading: Luke 18:1-14

Now Jesus was telling the disciples a parable to make the point that at all times they ought to pray and not give up *and* lose heart, ²saying, "In a certain city there was a judge who did not fear God and had no respect for man. ³There was a desperate widow in that city and she kept coming to him and saying, 'Give me justice *and* legal protection from my adversary.' ⁴For a time he would not; but later he said to himself, 'Even though I do not fear God nor respect man, ⁵yet because this widow *continues* to bother me, I will give her justice *and* legal protection; otherwise by continually coming she will be an intolerable annoyance and she will wear me out.'" ⁶Then the Lord said, "Listen to what the unjust judge says! ⁷And will not our just God defend *and* avenge His elect His chosen ones who cry out to Him day and night? Will He delay in providing justice on their behalf? ⁸I tell you that He will defend *and* avenge them quickly. However, when the Son of Man comes, will He find this kind of persistent faith on the earth?" ⁹He also told this parable to some people who trusted in themselves *and* were confident that they were righteous posing outwardly as upright and in right standing with God, and who viewed others with contempt: ¹⁰"Two men went up into the temple enclosure to pray, one a Pharisee and the other a tax collector. ¹¹The Pharisee stood and began praying to himself in a self-righteous way, saying: 'God, I thank You that I am not like the rest of men—swindlers, unjust, dishonest, adulterers—or even like this tax collector. ¹²I fast twice a week; I pay tithes of all that I get.' ¹³But the tax collector, standing at a distance, would not even raise his eyes toward heaven, but was striking his chest in humility and repentance, saying, 'God, be merciful *and* gracious to me, the especially wicked sinner that I am!' ¹⁴I tell you, this man went to his home forgiven of the guilt of sin and placed in right standing with God, justified; rather than the other man; for everyone who exalts himself will be humbled, but he who humbles himself will be exalted.

☐ ☐ ☐ ☐ ☐ ☐ ☐ ☐ (22)

Oh blessed Lord! How much I need
Your Light to guide me on my way!
So many hands that without heed still
touch Your wounds and make them

bleed, so many feet that day by day
still wander from Your fold astray!
Feeble at best is my endeavour! I see
but cannot reach the height that lies

forever in the Light; and yet forever and for ever, when seeming just within my grasp, I feel my feeble hands unclasp, and sink discouraged into night. For Your own purpose You have permitted the strife and the discouragement.[191]

Lord, what can I say? I am Yours. Keep me simply Yours. To my body, soul and spirit come with an influx of life. Lord, through all the multitudinous duties of the day keep me calm, ennobled by Your touch and tenderness. O Lord, it is You I want, strong and mighty and pure. Settle me and quieten me down in You. Your Word says, *cast all your cares upon Him, for He cares for you.* What a wonderful comfort those Words are! Lord, I look to You that I may be renewed my mind and spirit. How entirely I look to You! To You I come with great and glad expectancy. Cleanse me and keep me purely and calmly Yours. Gather me into concentrated peace in You.[192]

You clearly commend my unceasing dependence on You through the persistence of prayer and tenacity of sticking with the goals and pursuits established for me. May I be a person who is and who is seen to be reverent of God and caring for people. Please give me energy to keep me from wearing out and protect me from behaving only to make way for the expedient and the way of least resistance. I seek to be a conveyer and champion of justice, so help me Lord. O God have mercy on me, a sinner. I humble myself before You. Justify me on the merits of Jesus Christ and His righteousness, I pray. I need You and I will not give up needing You. So help me God.

Almighty and ever-blessed God, I thank You for Your love which You promised will follow me all the days of my life. I thank You that You inform my mind with Your divine truth and undergird my will with Your grace. I thank You for every evidence of Your Spirit's leading, and for all those little happenings which seem at the time no more than chance, yet afterwards appear to me as part of Your gracious and glorious plan for the education of my soul. O let me not refuse Your leading nor let me quench this light which You have kindled within me. But rather let me daily grow in grace and in the knowledge of Jesus Christ my Lord and Master.

I think not only of myself nor do I pray only for myself, as I seek Your presence. I remember before You all my brothers and sisters who need Your help. Especially tonight I think

---

[191] Henry Wadsworth Longfellow

[192] Oswald Chambers

of those who face great temptations, those who are faced with tasks too great for their powers, those who stand in any valley of decision, and those who are in debt or poverty. I think of those who are suffering the consequences of misdeeds long ago repented of, those who, by reason of early surroundings, have never had a fair chance in life; I think of all the family circles broken by death, of all missionaries of the Kingdom of Heaven in far away corners of the earth, and of those who lift high the Lamp of Truth in lonely places.

My Father, help me through this day to so live that I bring help to others. My I bring credit to the Name I bear and joy to those who love me, and to those who honour You. May I be cheerful when things go wrong, persevering when things are difficult, and serene when things are irritating. Enable me to be helpful to those experiencing difficulties. May I be kind to those in need; and sympathetic to those whose hearts are sad. Grant that nothing may make me lose my temper, nothing may take away my joy, nothing may ruffle my peace, and nothing may make me bitter towards anyone. So grant that tomorrow all those with whom I work, and all those whom I meet, may see in me the reflection of the Master, whose I am, and whom I seek to serve. This I ask for Your love's sake.[193]

Blessing and glory and wisdom and thanksgiving and honour and power and might be to You my God for ever and ever![194]

[193] William Barclay

[194] Revelation 7:12 (New Revised Standard Version)

Gospel Reading: Luke 18:15-30

Now they were also bringing their babies to Him, so that He would touch *and* bless them, and when the disciples noticed it, they *began* reprimanding them. [16]But Jesus called them to Himself, saying to the apostles, "Allow the children to come to Me, and do not forbid them, for the kingdom of God belongs to such as these. [17]I assure you *and* most solemnly say to you, whoever does not receive the kingdom of God with faith and humility like a child will not enter it at all." [18]A certain ruler asked Him, "Good Teacher, what shall I do to inherit eternal life?" [19]Jesus said to him, "Why do you call Me good? No one is essentially and morally good except God alone. [20]You know the commandments: 'Do not commit adultery, do not steal, do not testify falsely, honor your father and your mother.'" [21]He replied, "I have kept all these things from my youth." [22]When Jesus heard this, He said to him, "You still lack one thing; sell everything that you have and distribute the money to the poor, and you will have abundant treasure in heaven; and come, follow Me, become My disciple, believe and trust in Me and walk the same path of life that I walk." [23]But when he heard these things, he became very sad, for he was extremely rich. [24]Jesus looked at him and said, "How difficult it is for those who are wealthy to enter the kingdom of God! [25]For it is easier for a camel to go through the eye of a needle than for a rich man who places his faith in wealth or status to enter the kingdom of God." [26]And those who heard it said, "Then who can be saved?" [27]But He said, "The things that are impossible with people are possible with God." [28]Peter said, "Look, we have left all things—homes, families, businesses - and followed You." [29]And He said to them, "I assure you *and* most solemnly say to you, there is no one who has left house or wife or brothers or parents or children for the sake of the kingdom of God, [30]who will not receive many times as much in this present age and in the age to come, eternal life.

☐ ☐ ☐ ☐ ☐ ☐ ☐ ☐ (23)

May none of God's wonderful works keep silence, night or morning. Bright stars, high mountains, the depths of the seas, sources of rushing rivers: may all these break into song as I sing to Father, Son and Holy Spirit. May all the angels in the heavens reply: Amen! Amen! Amen! Power, praise, honour, eternal glory to God, the only giver of grace. Amen! Amen! Amen![195]

Before You O Lord all human hearts lie bare and open. I have no intention of hiding anything from You today that I have done or thought or imagined. You know and see it all. O Lord whose tender mercies are over Your works, humbly and sorrowfully I crave Your forgiveness for the sins of this day. For every weakening and defiling thought to which my mind has given harbour. For every word spoken in hastiness or passion, for every failure of self-control. For every stumbling-block which by deed or example I have set in another's way, for every opportunity lost, and for every blessing thanklessly received. Forgive me, too, for loitering feet and a procrastinating will. Grant O Lord that, as the days go by, Your Spirit may more and more rule in my heart, giving me victory over these and all other sinful ways. To Your loving guardianship, O holy Father, I commend all those who are dear to me. Be with all those who tonight are in any peril or distress. Be with every melancholic heart, in every stricken home, beside every bed of pain, giving to all the blessing of peace. Amen.[196]

For the children and youth of the world I pray, O Lord. I acknowledge that You declared that the kingdom of God belongs to the young and those whose attention is to care for babies, children and youth. I pray tonight for parents, guardians, care-givers, teachers, educators, social services and health care professionals and others who occupy their lives for the best interests of children . . . all precious in Your sight. For infants, children and youth at the margins of life, especially those subject to disease, war, poverty, abuse, poor nutrition and lack of shelter, be with those who directly care for these and supply their need for supply from the abundance of others.

Jesus, You have said *what is impossible for men and women is possible with God.* Displace my unbelief with an all-surrendering faith in You as the living, active, compassionate, just and personally engaged King of the kingdom. May I abandon attachments that inhibit my full reliance on Your soveign rule in my heart and life.

O Holy Spirit of God come into my heart and fill me. I open the windows of my soul to let You in. I surrender my whole life to You. Come and possess me, fill me with light and truth. I offer to You the one thing I really possess: My capacity for being filled by You. Of myself I am an unprofitable servant, an empty vessel. Fill me so that I may live the life of

[195] Source unknown, 3rd century (Egypt)

[196] Adapted from John Baillie, 1949

the Spirit: The life of truth and goodness, the life of beauty and love, the life of wisdom and strength. And guide me this week in all things. Lead me to the people I should meet or help. Lead me to the circumstances in which I can best serve You, whether by my action, or by my sufferings. But, above all, may Christ be formed in me. I dethrone myself and make Him king. Bind and cement me to Christ by all Your ways known and unknown, by holy thoughts, and unseen graces, and sacramental ties, so that You are in me, and I am in You, today, and forever.[197]

Fill me, with Your light and life, that I may show forth Your wondrous glory. Grant that Your love may so fill my life that I may count nothing too small to do for You, nothing too much to give, and nothing too hard to bear. Teach me, Lord, to serve You, as You deserve, to give and not to count the cost, to fight and not to heed the wounds, to toil and not to seek for rest, to labour and not to ask for any reward save that of knowing that I do Your will. Amen.[198]

From all that dwells below the skies, let the Creator's praise arise. Let the Redeemer's Name be sung through every land, in every tongue.

Eternal are Your mercies, Lord. Eternal truth attends Your Word. Your praise shall sound from shore to shore, til suns shall rise and set no more.[199]

---

[197] W. J. Carey

[198] Ignatius of Loyola

[199] Isaac Watts (1674-1748)

Gospel Reading: Luke 18:31-43

Then taking the twelve disciples aside, He said to them, "Listen carefully: we are going up to Jerusalem, and all things that have been written through the prophets about the Son of Man will be fulfilled *and* completed. ³²He will be betrayed *and* handed over to the Roman authorities, and will be mocked *and* ridiculed and insulted *and* abused and spit on, ³³and after they have scourged Him, they will kill Him; and on the third day He will rise from the dead." ³⁴But the disciples understood none of these things about the approaching death and resurrection of Jesus. This statement was hidden from them, and they did not grasp the meaning of the things that were said by Jesus. ³⁵As He was approaching Jericho on His way to Jerusalem, it happened that a blind man was sitting beside the road begging. ³⁶Now when he heard a crowd going by, he *began* to ask what this was about. ³⁷They told him, "Jesus of Nazareth is passing by." ³⁸So he shouted out, saying, "Jesus, Son of David have mercy on me!" ³⁹Those who were leading the way were sternly telling him to keep quiet; but he screamed all the more, "Son of David, have mercy on me!" ⁴⁰Then Jesus stopped and ordered that the blind man be led to Him; and when he came near, Jesus asked him, ⁴¹"What do you want Me to do for you?" He said, "Lord, let me regain my sight!" ⁴²Jesus said to him, "Regain your sight; your personal trust and confident faith in Me has made you well." ⁴³Immediately he regained his sight and *began* following Jesus, glorifying *and* praising *and* honoring God. And all the people, when they saw it, praised God.

 (24)

With amazing precision, what was prophesized in the Old Testament about the Son of Man was fulfilled: Culminating in Your brutal death but celebrated in Your glorious resurrection. Thank You for coming to seek and to save the lost. Thank You, O Great Physician, for Your lifegiving compassion. I come as a beggar to the Owner and Ruler of the universe and say to You: *Have mercy on me, I want to see.* Thank You for hearing my prayer, may I see with eyes of faith and may I forever praise Your Name, Jesus of Nazareth, Son of David, my God and my Saviour.

To You, O Jesus, I turn. You are the River of Life who alone can satisfy my thirst. Without You all else is barren and void. Without all else You alone are enough for me. You are the Redeemer of those who are lost; the sweet Consoler of the sorrowful and the Crown of Glory for the victors. You are the Recompense of the blessed day when I hope to receive of Your fullness, and to sing the song of praise in my true home. Give me only a few drops of consolation and I will patiently wait Your coming that I may enter into Your joy my Lord.[200] I am no longer my own but Yours. Put me to what You will. Put me to doing. Put me to suffering. Let me be employed for You, be laid aside for You, be exalted for You, or be brought low for You. Let me be full, let me be empty. Let me have all things, let me have nothing. I freely and wholeheartedly yield all things to Your pleasure and disposal. And now glorious and blessed God, Father, Son and Holy Spirit, You are mine and I am Yours. So be it. And this covenant, now made on earth, let it be satisfied in Heaven. Amen.[201]

In the Name of Jesus Christ, who was never in a hurry, I pray, O God, that You will slow me down, for I know that I live too fast. If I am to burn myself out, may it be in causes worth dying for. With all of eternity before me, may I take the time to get acquainted with You, leave time to enjoy Your blessings, and take time to get to know the people around me better. Deliver me from wasting time and teach me how to use my gifts wisely and well. Father, I have a great need of Your guidance. I know that by myself I am not sufficient for these days and that the problems in my small part of the world are beyond the measure of my best wisdom. Lord Jesus, You promised that by faith Your disciples might remove mountains. Please increase my faith, till I no longer am stymied by difficulties and frightened by problems. Hold me and those I love by Your mighty hand until doubts cease and I begin to believe afresh. As I fall into sleep may I find all things possible and for tomorrow give me your solutions to the questions that perplex me. For this I pray. Amen.[202]

I know Father that there is a time to speak and a time to keep silence. Help me to tell the one from the other. When I should speak, give me the courage of my convictions. When I should keep silence, restrain me from speaking, lest, in my desire to appear wise, I give myself away. Teach me the sacraments of silence, that I may use these to know myself, and, above me, to know You. Then shall I be wise. In the face of life's mysteries and

[200] Bonaventure, 1221-74

[201] John Wesley

[202] Adapted from Peter Marshall (1902–67)

its vast imponderables, give me faith to believe that You make all things to work together for good to those who love You and those who are called according to Your purposes. Strengthen my conviction that Your hand is upon me, to lead me and to use me in working out Your purposes in the world. Even though I may not see the distant scene and circumstances, let me be willing to take one step at a time and trust You for the rest, through Jesus Christ my Lord. Amen.[203]

O Holy Spirit, Love of God, powerful Advocate and sweetest Comforter, infuse Your grace and descend plentifully into my heart. Father and the Son come likewise and inhabit me. O come, Cleanser of all inward pollutions, and Healer of spiritual wounds and diseases. Come, in much mercy, and make me fit to receive You.[204]

---

[203] Adapted from Peter Marshall (1902–67)

[204] Saint Augustine

Gospel Reading: Luke 19:1-10

Jesus entered Jericho and was passing through. ²And there was a man called Zaccheus; he was a chief tax collector, a superintendent to whom others reported, and he was rich. ³Zaccheus was trying to see who Jesus was, but he could not see because of the crowd, for he was short in stature. ⁴So he ran on ahead of the crowd and climbed up in a sycamore tree in order to see Him, for He was about to pass through that way. ⁵When Jesus reached the place, He looked up and said to him, "Zaccheus, hurry and come down, for today I must stay at your house." ⁶So Zaccheus hurried and came down, and welcomed Jesus with joy. ⁷When the people saw it, they all *began* muttering in discontent, "He has gone to be the guest of a man who is a notorious sinner." ⁸Zaccheus stopped and said to the Lord, "See, Lord, I am now giving half of my possessions to the poor, and if I have cheated anyone out of anything, I will give back four times as much." ⁹Jesus said to him, "Today salvation has come to this household, because he, too, is a spiritual son of Abraham; ¹⁰for the Son of Man has come to seek and to save that which was lost.

 (25)

O unapproachable Light, how can I fold these guilty hands before You? How can I pray to You with lips that have spoken false and churlish words? A heart hardened with vindictive passions: an unruly tongue, a fretful disposition, an unwillingness to bear the burdens of others, an undue willingness to let others bear my burdens, high professions joined to low attainments, fine words hiding shabby thoughts, a friendly face masking a cold heart, many neglected opportunities and many uncultivated talents, much love and beauty unappreciated and many blessings unacknowledged. All these I confess to You, O God. I thank You, O loving Father, that, holy and transcendent as You are, You have through all the ages shown Yourself to be accessible to the prayers of erring mortals such as me. I praise Your Name that in the Gospel of Jesus Christ You have opened up a new and living way into Your presence, making Your mercy free to all who have nothing else to plead.

Let me now find peace of heart by fleeing from myself and taking refuge in You. Let despair over my miserable sins give place to joy in

Your adorable goodness. Let depression of mind make way for renewed zeal and for the spirit of service. So let me lie down tonight thinking, not of myself and my own affairs, or of my own hopes and fears, or even of my own sins in Your sight, but of others who need Your help and of the work that I can do for their sakes in the vineyard of Your world.[205] Our Father in heaven, may Your Name be hallowed. Your kingdom come; Your will be done, on earth as in heaven. Give me this night my daily bread. Forgive me the wrong I have done, as I have forgiven those who have wronged me. And do not put me to the test, but deliver me and those I love from the evil one.[206] Lord, whatever this night may bring, Your Name be praised.[207]

I look forward to the day when I will see You face to face Lord Jesus. You are Love Incarnate and Author of my life. There will be a day when I shall know fully even as I have been fully known.[208] I welcome You to be with me tonight O Lord. May I do as You will and participate fully in Your kingdom purposes. I owe You everything; You own all. Help me to be a good steward of all You've given.

Help me to be a person of integrity for Your Name sake.

How easy, Lord, it is for me to live with You. How easy it is for me to believe in You. When my understanding is perplexed by doubts or at the point of giving up, when I see no further than the coming morning, and know not what I will do tomorrow, You send me a clear assurance that You are with me and that You will ensure that not all the roads of goodness are barred. I look back in wonder at the road that led through hopelessness to this place from where I can reflect Your radiance. And whatever I in this life may yet reflect, You will give me. And whatever I shall not attain, that, plainly, You have purposed for others.[209]

Dear Jesus, help me to spread Your fragrance everywhere I go. Flood my soul with Your spirit and life. Penetrate and possess my whole being, so utterly, that my life may only be a radiance of Yours. Shine through me, and be so in me, that every person I come in contact with may feel Your presence. Let them look up and see no longer me, but only Jesus! Stay with me, and then I shall begin to shine as You shine, to shine as a light to others.[210]

[205] Adapted from John Baillie, 1949

[206] Matthew 6.9-13 (Revised English Bible)

[207] Dietrich Bonhoeffer (Written while awaiting execution in a Nazi prison)

[208] 1 Corinthians 13:12

[209] Alexander Solzhenitsyn

[210] John Henry Newman

Come, my Light, and illumine my darkness. Come, my Life, and revive me from death. Come, my Physician, and heal my wounds. Come, Flame of divine love, and burn up the thorns of my sins, kindling my heart with the flame of Your love. Come, my King, sit upon the throne of my heart and reign there. For You alone are my King and my Lord.[211]

---

[211] Saint Imitri of Rastov

Gospel Reading: Luke 19:11-27

While they were listening to these things, Jesus went on to tell a parable, because He was near Jerusalem, and they assumed that the kingdom of God was going to appear immediately as soon as He reached the city. [12]So He said, "A nobleman went to a distant country to obtain for himself a kingdom, and then to return. [13]So he called ten of his servants, and gave them ten minas, each equal to about a hundred days' wages, and said to them, 'Do business with this until I return.' [14]But the residents of his new kingdom hated him and sent a delegation after him, saying, 'We do not want this man to be a king over us.' [15]When he returned, after receiving the kingdom, he ordered that these servants, to whom he had given the money, be called to him, that he might find out what business they had done. [16]The first one came before him and said, 'Lord, your mina has made ten more minas.' [17]And he said to him, 'Well done, good servant! Because you proved yourself faithful *and* trustworthy in a very little thing, you shall now have authority over ten cities in my kingdom.' [18]The second one came and said, 'Lord, your mina has made five minas.' [19]And he said to him also, 'And you shall take charge over five cities.' [20]Then another came and said, 'Lord, here is your mina, which I have kept laid up in a handkerchief for safekeeping. [21]I was always afraid of you, because you are a stern man; you pick up what you did not lay down and you reap what you did not sow.' [22]He said to the servant, 'I will judge *and* condemn you by your own words, you worthless servant! Did you really know that I was a stern man, picking up what I did not lay down and reaping what I did not sow? [23]Then why did you not at the very least put my money in a bank? Then on my return, I would have collected it with interest.' [24]Then he said to the bystanders, 'Take the mina away from him and give it to the one who has the ten minas.' [25]And they said to him, 'Lord, he has ten minas *already*!' [26]Jesus explained, 'I tell you that to everyone who has because he valued his gifts from God and has used them wisely, *more* will be given; but from the one who does not have because he disregarded his gifts from God, even what he has will be taken away.' [27]The king ended by saying, 'But as for these enemies of mine who did not want me to be king over them, bring them here and kill them in my presence.'

 (26)

As I wait for Your return O Coming King, may Your kingdom come on earth as it is in heaven. Give me patience as I wait and direct my path to do Your will and to be an excellent, even exceptional, steward of the gifts You've given to me to invest. I long to hear from You, the words: *Well done my good and trustworthy servant*. May I, in small matters and large, be found faithful. May my words and actions be full of integrity and without disappointment to You. As Your servant I ask that You would give me the wisdom and wherewithal to please You, to glorify and honour You, with all my heart and strength. Move me beyond mere intention to action and to obedience as I trust You and experience the unction of Your Holy Spirit in my life.

O merciful heart of God, in true penitence and contrition, I would now open my heart to You. Let me keep nothing hidden from You while I pray. As humbling as the truth about myself may be, let me take courage to speak it in Your presence. In Your wisdom use this pain of confession as a means to make me hate the sins confessed. I confess to the sin of laziness. I confess to the sin of vanity. I confess to indulgence of the flesh. I confess to the habit of falsehood. I confess to

dishonesty. I confess to uncharitable words. I confess to harbouring evil thoughts. I confess to the wrong directions I have taken in my life through poor decisions. I confess to lapses from faithful practicing of Your presence and my dependence on You. May Your love be so at work in my heart as a fire to burn up all that is shameful and evil, let me now lay hold upon Your perfect righteousness and make it mine through Jesus Christ's efficacious work on the cross. Blot out all my transgressions and let my sins be covered. Help me to feel Your hand upon my life, cleansing me from the stains of past misdeeds, releasing me from the grip of evil habits, strengthening me in new habits of pure-heartedness, and guiding my footsteps in the way of eternal life. Lead me in battle, O God, against my secret sins. Fence my life with pure aspirations. And let Christ be formed in my heart through faith. All this I ask for Your holy Name's sake. Amen.[212]

O God, my Father, I see that when problems come I need not whine or complain. I can make music out of misery, a song out of sorrow and success out of every setback. I feel sad when I think of the number of times I have failed to thank those through

---

[212] Adapted from John Baillie, 1949

whom Your blessings have come into my life – Your agents. From now on I must be more sensitive and alert. Help me, dear Father. And forgive me for going through this day overlooking the common blessings of life. Help me to develop keen sight so that I do not miss one of the benefits You have given to me. Give me a thankful heart, dear Lord. What will You give me this week that I might offer back to You in thanksgiving, in praise and adoration? Help me not to miss one single thing. In Jesus' Name. Amen.[213]

Let us make our way together, Lord; wherever You go I must go and through whatever You pass, there too I will pass.[214] Lord, let me not live to be useless.[215] May Your strength O God pilot me. May Your power O God preserve me. May Your wisdom O God instruct me. May Your hand O God protect me. May Your way O God direct me. May Your shield O God defend me. And may Your heavenly army O God guard me against the snares of evil and the temptations of the world.[216]

Father in heaven, I give thanks for the experiences that life brings me. I thank You for my joys, sorrows, trials, failures and triumphs. Above all, I thank You for the hope I have in Christ. I thank You that I find fulfilment in Him. I praise You for my country, its beauty, the riches it has for all of us and the gifts it showers on us. I thank You for Your People, the gift of languages spoken, the variety of people we have in our midst, the cultural and ethnic heritages we cherish and the latent possibilities there are for this country to be a great blessing to other people and places on this globe. Grant that I accept these gifts with thankfulness, and use them for the good of the entire human race and to bring glory to You, through Jesus Christ my Lord. Amen.[217]

[213] Selwyn Hughes

[214] Teresa of Avila, 1515-82

[215] John Wesley, 1703-91

[216] Patrick, c.389-c.461

[217] Source unknown (India)

Gospel Reading: Luke 19:28-40

After saying these things, Jesus went on ahead of them, going up to Jerusalem. [29]When He approached Bethphage and Bethany, at the mount that is called Olivet, He sent two of the disciples, [30]saying, "Go into the village ahead of you; there, as you enter, you will find a donkey's colt tied, on which no one has ever sat. Untie it and bring it here. [31]If anybody asks you, 'Why are you untying the colt?' you will say, 'The Lord needs it.'" [32]So those who were sent left and found the colt just as He had told them. [33]As they were untying the colt, its owners asked them, "Why are you untying the colt?" [34]They said, "The Lord needs it." [35]They brought it to Jesus, and they threw their robes over the colt and put Jesus on it. [36]As He rode along, people were spreading their coats on the road, as an act of homage before a king. [37]As soon as He was approaching Jerusalem, near the descent of the Mount of Olives, the entire multitude of the disciples, all those who were or claimed to be His followers, began praising God adoring Him enthusiastically and joyfully with loud voices for all the miracles *and* works of power that they had seen, [38]shouting, "Blessed is the King who comes in the name of the Lord! Peace in heaven and glory, majesty, and splendor in the highest heaven!" [39]Some of the Pharisees from the crowd said to Him, "Teacher, rebuke Your disciples for shouting these Messianic praises." [40]Jesus replied, "I tell you, if these people keep silent, the stones will cry out in praise!

 (27)

Hosanna, blessed are You King Jesus, the heavens and the earth declare Your glory. O, the depth of the riches of the wisdom and knowledge of God! How unsearchable Your judgements, and Your paths beyond tracing out! Who has known Your mind? Or who has been Your counselor? Who has ever given to You that You should repay? For from You and through You, and to You are all things. To You King Jesus be the glory forever.[218] I worship You for Your triumph over sin, Satan and death. I praise You for Your saving and sanctifying love. I honour You for the glory of Your Name.

Now, O Lord, as the day's work is done, I turn once more to You. From You all things come, in You I live, and in You all things end. You are both Alpha and Omega, the beginning and the end. In the morning

---

[218] Romans 11:33-36

I set out with Your blessing; all day You have upheld me by Your grace, and now I pray that You will grant me rest and peace. I cast all my cares upon You and leave to You the outcomes of my labour. I ask You to prosper all that has been done today in accordance with Your will. Please forgive me for all that has been done amiss. If I have done any harm, annul and overrule it by Your almighty power.

O Lord, I remember before You tonight all the workers of the world. I pray for those who work with hands and those who work with heads; workers in cities and in the fields, men and women who toil, both employers and employees. I pray for those who supervise and those who sweat, those whose work is dangerous, those whose work is monotonous; those who can find no work, those whose work is the service of the poor or the healing of the sick or the proclamation of the Gospel of Christ. O Christ, who came not to be ministered to but to minister, have mercy upon all who labour faithfully to serve the common good. O Christ, You fed the hungry multitude with loaves and fishes, have mercy upon all who labour to earn their daily bread. O Christ, You called to Yourself all those who labour and are heavy laden, have mercy upon all whose work is beyond their strength.

And to You, with the Father and the Holy Spirit, be all the glory and the praise. Amen.[219]

O GOD, You loved me so much that You sent Jesus Christ for the illumination of my darkness and the salvation of my soul; give me wisdom to profit by the Words He spoke, faith to accept the salvation He offers, and grace to follow in His steps. As You, Christ, said: *When you stand praying, forgive, if you have a complaint against any*, O God, give me grace now so to do. As You, Christ, said: *It is more blessed to give than to receive*, O God, give me grace tonight to think, not of what I can get, but of what I can give. As, You, Christ said: *Judge not, that you be not judged*, O God, give me grace to first to cast out the log out of my own eye before I regard the sliver of wood that is in my sister's or brothers' eye. And when I find it hard to be humble, hard to forgive, O Lord, remind me how much harder it was to hang on the cross.[220]

Almighty Father, King of kings and queens and Lord of all rulers, grant that the hearts and minds of all who serve as leaders, as statespersons, as judges, as people of learning, and as persons of wealth, may be so filled with the love of Your laws, and of that

---

[219] Adapted from John Baillie, 1949
[220] Adapted from Peter Marshall (1902–67)

which is righteous and life-giving, that
they may serve as worthy stewards of
Your good and perfect gifts, through
Jesus Christ our Lord.[221] Almighty
God, You are the exclusive holder of
eternal power, and all other people's
power is but borrowed from You. I
call upon You for all those who hold
office that they may use their positions
for the general good and bring You
honour to You, through Jesus Christ
their Lord and mine.[222]

You have called me to be holy.
You have sent the Advocate to stand
beside me in my trials. O Divine
Master, call me ever more powerfully
to follow You in the way of holiness.
Call me to sanctification by Your life
and death, by Your Word and by Your
resurrection power that works in and
through me, by Your Holy Spirit.
Make me, by Your grace, a witness to
Your salvation and holiness in this
world, guided by the light shining
from Your Cross.[223]

[221] Source unknown, 1348 (Prayer of the Order of the Garter)

[222] William Tyndale, c.1494-1536 (adapted

[223] Benedict Groeschel (Quiet Moments)

Gospel Reading: Luke 19:41-47

As He approached *Jerusalem*, He saw the city and wept over the spiritual ignorance of its people, [42]saying, "If only you had known on this day of salvation, even you, the things which make for peace and on which peace depends! But now they have been hidden from your eyes. [43]For a time of siege is coming when your enemies will put up a barricade with pointed stakes against you, and surround you with armies and hem you in on every side, [44]and they will level you to the ground, you - Jerusalem - and your children within you. They will not leave in you one stone on another, all because you did not come progressively to recognize from observation and personal experience the time of your visitation when God was gracious toward you and offered you salvation." [45]Jesus went into the temple enclosure and began driving out those who were selling, [46]saying to them, "It is written, 'My house shall be a house of prayer'; but you have made it a robbers' den." [47]He was teaching day after day in the temple porches and courts; but the chief priests and scribes and the leading men among the people were seeking a way to put Him to death.

 (28)

O Divine Love, You everlastingly stand outside the closed doors of the souls of men and women, boys and girls, knocking ever and again. Give me grace to throw open all my soul's doors and let every bolt and bar be drawn that has robbed my life of air and light and love. Give me an open ear, O God, that I may hear Your voice calling me to high endeavour. Too often have I been deaf to the appeals You have addressed to me, but now give me courage to answer, *Here am I, send m*e. And when any one of Your children cries out in need, give me then an open ear to hear in that cry Your call to service. Give me an open mind, O God, a mind ready to receive and to welcome such new light of knowledge as it is Your will to reveal to me. Let not the past ever be so dear to me as to set a limit to the future. Give me courage to change my mind, when that is needed. Let me be tolerant to the thoughts of others and hospitable to such light as may come to me through them. Give me open eyes, O God, eyes quick to discover Your indwelling in the world. Let all lovely things fill me with gladness and let them uplift my mind to Your everlasting loveliness. Forgive all my past blindness to the grandeur and glory of nature, to the charm of little children, to the sublimities of human story, and to all the intimations of Your presence which these things contain. Give me open hands, O God, hands ready to share with all who are in want of the blessings. Deliver me from all meanness and miserliness. Let me hold money in stewardship and all worldly goods in trust for You, to whom now be all honour and glory. Amen.[224]

Jesus, You know the beginning and the ending. You know my sitting, my standing and my deepest of thoughts, even before I am conscious of them. You have every hair in my head counted and You care deeply for me. This knowledge and intimate understanding is too much for me to contain. Because of Your compassion, Your desire for friendshipyou're your companionship, I am afforded incredible dignity and I am made in Your image and likeness. Made for You. You see each person and each community in this way and You feel each high point, each pain and You both rejoice and weep. May I increasingly regard the sacridity of our relationship and our friendship with due respect. May I do everything possible to appreciate and set apart my life for worship and enjoyment of You – such that You are glorified.

O God, grant me in all my duties Your help, in all my perplexities Your guidance, in all my dangers Your protection, and in all my sorrows Your peace.[225] Almighty God, give me wisdom to perceive You, intellect to understand You, diligence to seek You, patience to wait for You, eyes to behold You, a heart to meditate upon You and life to proclaim You, through the power of the Spirit of my Lord Jesus Christ.[226]

My Lord God, I have no idea where I am going. I do not see the road ahead of me. I cannot know for certain where it will end. Nor do I really know myself, and the fact that I think I am following Your will does not mean that I am actually doing so. But I believe that the desire to please You does in fact please You, and I hope that I have that desire in all that I am doing. I hope that I never do anything apart from that desire. And I know that if I do this You will lead me by the right road though I may know nothing about it. Therefore I will trust You always. Though I may seem to be lost and in the shadow of death I will not fear, for You are ever with me and

[224] Adapted from John Baillie, 1949

[225] Augustine, 354-430
[226] Benedict, 480-543

You will never leave me to face my peril alone.[227]

Preserve me, O most holy Lord God, from the cares of this life; that my feet be not entangled by them and deliver me from spiritual hindrances and temptations, that I am not wearied and cast down. Let not the world and the things of the world deceive me and keep me from the power and malice of the devil. Confirm me in Your Ways, O Lord, by the grace of Your Holy Spirit. Strengthen me with might, so that no trouble or temptation may draw me away from You.[228]

---

[227] Thomas Merton

[228] Thomas A Kempis

Gospel Reading: Luke 20:1-8

On one of the days, as Jesus was instructing the people in the temple area and preaching the good news of the gospel, the chief priests and the scribes along with the elders confronted *Him*, ²and said to Him, "Tell us by what *kind of* authority You are doing these things? Or who is the one who gave You this authority?" ³Jesus replied, "I will also ask you a question. You tell Me: ⁴The baptism of John the Baptist—was it from heaven and ordained by God or from men?" ⁵They discussed *and* debated it among themselves, saying, "If we say, 'From heaven,' He will say, 'Why did you not believe him?' ⁶But if we say, 'From men,' all the people will stone us to death, for they are *firmly* convinced that John was a prophet." ⁷So they replied that they did not know from where *it* came. ⁸Then Jesus said to them, "Nor am I telling you by what kind of authority I do these things.

 (29)

My God, how wonderful You are, Your majesty how bright! How beautiful Your mercy-seat, in depths of burning light! How dread are Your eternal years, O everlasting Lord, by prostrate spirit day and night incessantly adored! How beautiful, how beautiful the sight of You must be, Your endless wisdom, boundless power and awful purity! O how I fear You, living God, with deepest and tenderest fears, and worship You with trembling hope and penitential tears! Yet I may love You, too, O Lord, Almighty as You are, for You have stooped to ask of me the love of my poor heart. No earthly father loves me like You; no mother, was ever so mild, bears and forbears as You have done with me, Your sinful child. Father of

Jesus, love's reward, what rapture will it be prostrate before Your throne be and gaze and gaze on You.[229]

God of the whole earth, King of kings, Prince of Peace, I worship You in the beauty of Your holiness this evening. All authority in heaven and earth are Yours. Jesus Christ, You, in unity with the Father and the Spirit are One: Creator, Sustainer and Redeemer. I worship You; I praise Your Name. You are above all others. You are all powerful, all knowing and are ever present. Your compassion never fails; You have never lost a battle; You have never broken a promise; and You, mighty God, love me with an intimate deep and abiding

---

[229] Frederick William Faber (1814-1863)

love. O sacrificing and wonderful Saviour, I worship You and say I love You.

To You, Creator of nature and humanity, Creator of truth and beauty, I pray: Hear the voice of the victims of all wars and violence among individuals and nations. Hear all the children who suffer and will suffer when people put their faith in weapons and war. I beg You to instil into the hearts of all human beings the wisdom of peace, the strength of justice and the joy of fellowship. Multitudes in every country, who do not want war and are ready to walk the road of peace, call out to You Lord. Hear our voices and grant insight and strength so that I, with others, may always respond to hatred with love, to injustice with total dedication to justice, to need with the sharing of self, and to war with peace. O God, hear my voice, and grant to the world Your everlasting peace.[230]

O God, You and You alone are all-wise and all knowing! You know just what is best for me. You love me better than I love myself. You are all-wise and all-powerful. I thank You, with all my heart, that You have taken me out of my own keeping, and have invited me to put myself in Your hands. I ask to be in Your care and not my own. O my Lord, through Your grace, I will follow You whereever You go. I will wait on You for Your guidance, and, on obtaining it, I will act without fear. And I promise that I will not be impatient, if at any time I am kept by You in darkness and perplexity; nor will I complain or fret if I come into any misfortune or anxiety. Amen.[231]

O Lord, breathe on me with that breath which infuses energy and kindles fervour. In asking for fervour, I ask for all that I need, and all that You will give. In asking for fervour, I am asking for faith, hope, and love, in their most heavenly exercise; I am asking for perception of duty, I am asking for sanctity, peace, and joy, all at once. Nothing would be a trouble to me, nothing a difficulty, had I but a fervour of soul. Lord, in asking for fervour, I am asking for Yourself, for I need nothing short of You, Yourself, O my God. Enter my heart, and fill me with fervour by filling me with Yourself. Amen.[232]

Gracious and Holy Father, continue to give me wisdom to perceive You, intelligence to understand You, diligence to seek You, patience to wait for You, eyes to behold You, a heart to meditate upon

[230] (Pope) John Paul 11

[231] John Henry Newman

[232] John Henry Newman

You, and a life to proclaim You,
through the power of the Holy Spirit
of Jesus Christ, my Lord.[233]

[233] Saint Benedict

Gospel Reading: Luke 20:9-19

Then He began to tell the people this parable: "A man planted a vineyard and leased it to tenant farmers, and went on a journey for a long time to another country. ¹⁰At *harvest* time he sent a servant as his representative to the tenants, so that they would give him *his share* of the fruit of the vineyard; but the tenants beat the servant and sent him away empty-handed. ¹¹So he again sent another servant; they also beat him and dishonored *and* treated him disgracefully and sent him away empty-handed. ¹²And he sent yet a third; and this one too they wounded and threw out of the vineyard. ¹³Then the owner of the vineyard said, 'What shall I do? I will send my beloved son; perhaps they will have respect for him.' ¹⁴But when the tenants saw him, they discussed it among themselves, saying, 'This man is the heir; let us kill him so that the inheritance will be ours.' ¹⁵So they threw the son out of the vineyard and killed him. What, then, will the owner of the vineyard do to them? ¹⁶He will come and put these tenants to death and will give the vineyard to others." When the chief priests, the scribes, and the elders heard this, they said, "May it never be!" ¹⁷But Jesus looked at them and said, "What then is the meaning of this that is written: 'The very stone which the builders rejected, this became the chief cornerstone'? ¹⁸Everyone who falls on that stone will be broken *and* shattered in pieces; and on whomever it falls, it will crush him." ¹⁹The scribes and the chief priests tried to find a way to arrest Him at that very hour, but they were afraid of the people; because they understood that He spoke this parable against them.

☐ ☐ ☐ ☐ ☐ ☐ ☐ ☐ (30)

O Ruler of the universe have mercy on me, a sinner. You are the owner of all and I am Your servant. You are the foundation of my life; You hold the whole world together by the power of Your Word. I revere You and those You have anointed and set apart. May I be an able discerner between the sacred and the profane. Give me a holy respect for all that I ought to honour. It is my desire to abide in You. I want to be graphed into Your ways and I long for You to be fully in me, as I yield my life to You. May the explanation of my life be summed up as Christ in me, the hope of glory. Renovate my heart and cause my life to thrive and overflow to the benefit of others and to Your eternal glory, through Jesus Christ. Amen.

Almighty God, in this hour of quiet I seek communion with You. From the fret and fever of the day's business, from the world's discordant noises, from the praise and blame of people, from the confused thoughts and vain imaginations of my own heart, I now turn aside and seek the quietness of Your presence. All day long have I expended energy and striven; but now, as I still my heart and in the clear light of Your eternity, I ponder the pattern that my life has been weaving. May there fall upon me now, O God, a great sense of Your power and Your glory, so that I see all earthly things and efforts in their true measure. With You a thousand years is as one day. Give me an understanding of Your perfect holiness so that all pride in my own attainment is displaced. Grant me a vision of Your untreated beauty as makes me dissatisfied with all lesser beauties.

O Father, I put my life in Your hands, believing that You have every hair on my head numbered. I am content to give over my will to Your control, believing that I can find in You a righteousness that I could never have won for myself. I am content to leave all my dear ones to Your care, believing that Your love for them is greater than my own. I am content to leave in Your hands the causes of truth and of justice, and the coming of Your Kingdom to the hearts of women and men, believing that my care is but a feeble shadow of Your purpose and loving intentions. To You, O God, be glory for ever. Amen.[234]

Heavenly Father, I commend to Your mercy those for whom life does not spell freedom: prisoners of conscience, the homeless and the disabled, the sick in body and mind, the elderly who are confined to their homes, those who are enslaved by their passions, and those who are addicted to drugs. Grant that, whatever their outward circumstances, each may find inward freedom, through Him who proclaimed release to captives, Jesus Christ our Saviour.[235]

Lord, I pray this night mindful of the sorry confusion of our world. Look with mercy upon this generation of Your children: so steeped in misery of our own contriving, so far strayed from Your ways and so blinded by world-anchored passions. I pray for the victims of tyranny, that they may resist oppression with courage. I pray for wicked and cruel, whose arrogance reveals to me what the sin of my own heart is like when it has conceived and

[234] Adapted from John Baillie, 1949

[235] John Stott

brought forth its final fruit. I pray for myself and my family that we might live in peace and quietness, that we may not regard our good life circumstances as proof of our virtue, or rest content to have our ease at the price of other people's sorrow and tribulation. I pray for all who have a vision of Your will, despite the confusions and betrayals of human sin, that they may humbly and resolutely plan for and fashion the foundations of a just peace between peoples, even while they seek to preserve what is fair and just among us, against the threat of malignant powers.[236]

Lord Jesus, cause me to know in my daily experience the glory and sweetness of Your Name, and then teach me how to pray. Your Name is my passport and secures my access. Your Name is my honour and secures me glory. Blessed Name, You are honey in my mouth, music in my ear, heaven in my heart, and all in all to my being.[237] I love You Lord Jesus Christ!

[236] Reinhold Niebuhr, 1892-1971

[237] C. H. Spurgeon

Reading: Luke 20:20-26

So they watched for a chance to trap Him. They sent spies who pretended to be upright *and* sincere, in order that they might catch Him in some statement that they could distort and use against Him, so that they could turn Him over to the control and authority of Pilate the governor. [21]They asked Him, "Teacher, we know that You speak and teach correctly, and that You show no partiality to anyone, but teach the way of God truthfully. [22]Is it lawful, according to Jewish law and tradition, for us to pay taxes to Caesar or not?" [23]But He saw through their trickery and said to them, [24]"Show Me a Roman denarius. Whose image and inscription does the coin have?" They answered, "the Emperor Tiberius Caesar's." [25]He said to them, "Then pay to Caesar the things that are Caesar's, and to God the things that are God's." [26]They were not able to seize on anything He said in the presence of the people; and being unnerved at His reply, they were silent.

 (31)

O Lord, my Lord, You decided before creation that all peoples, whatever their colour or race, are equal before You. Break down the hatred between tribes and peoples, especially hatred due to national and ethnic differences. I ask that You reconcile us to one another, so that each of us may respect the rights of others. I ask all this in the Name of my Saviour, Jesus Christ.[238]

Lord God of truth, save me from pretending; I am not good at it. My duplicity and my episodic and diminished integrity ends up depressing me. But You, Lord Jesus, being of the very nature and form of God, did not consider equality with God something to be grasped but You made Yourself nothing, taking on the very nature and form of a servant, being made in human likeness, You humbled Yourself and became obedient to death, even death on a Cross.[239] You see my hypocrisy; help me to grow in humility and follow You by way of the Cross. Lord You are unfoolable and brilliant in all Your ways. Lead me, love me, watch over me, and fill me so that You are the explanation for who I am becoming and for my authentic ways.

[238] Student Christian Movement (Zambia)

[239] Philippians 2:6-18

Gracious Father, so often I am confused and seem to live at cross-purposes to my central aims and to the interests of others. Tomorrow, take me by the hand and help me to see things from Your viewpoint, that I may see issues, circumstances, threats, problems and opportunities as they really are. May I come to choices and decisions with a prayer upon my lips; for my own wisdom fails me. Give me Your wisdom; that I may do Your will. As I reflect back on this day, I have long known that there is a time to speak and a time to keep silence. Help me to tell the one from the other. When I should speak, give me the courage of my convictions. When I should keep silence, restrain me from speaking. Let me embark on no undertaking that is not in line and on track with Your will for me. Illumine my mind and direct my thinking and my dreaming, that my thoughts and my actions tomorrow may merit Your blessing.[240]

O God, whose longing is to reconcile the whole universe inside Your love, pour out Your abundant mercy on Your Church, and on Your world, so fragmented and torn apart. For the long history of pain and travail, of oppression and prejudice inflicted on women, within the Church and in the world, *O God forgive us and pour out your mercy.* For my own failure to be open and responsive to the possibility of new freedom and new hopes, *O God forgive me and pour out Your mercy.* For my failure to resist the bitterness which poisons and sours the gospel of love and reconciliation, *O God forgive me and pour out Your mercy.* For my failure to present a wounded world with hope for reconciliation in a true and loving community of women and men, *O God forgive me and pour out Your mercy.*[241]

Grant, O Lord, favourable weather, peaceful showers, beneficent dews, and abundance of fruits. Remember, O Lord, all who bring forth fruit, and labour honourably in the services of Your Church and in the public square. Be mindful of all those who act for the good of the poor, the widows, the orphans, the strangers, the needy, and all who have remembered them in their prayers.[242] Come, Lord, and cover me with the night. Spread Your grace over me as You assure me You will do. Your promises are more than all the stars in the sky; Your mercy is deeper than the night. Lord, it will be cold. The night comes with its breath of death. Night comes; the end

---

[240] Adapted from Peter Marshall (1902–67)

[241] Source unknown (From the service of rejoicing for the fortieth anniversary of the ordination of Florence Li Tim Oi, Sheffield Cathedral, January 1984)

[242] Liturgy of Saint James

comes; You come. Lord, I wait for You day and night.[243]

You are worthy, my Lord and God, to receive glory and honour and power, for You created all things, and by Your will they were created and have their being.[244] Glory be to the Father and to the Son and to the Holy Spirit. As it was in the beginning is now and ever shall be, world without end.[245]

[243] Traditional Ghanian Prayer

[244] Revelation 4:11 (New International Version)

[245] Source unknown

Gospel Reading: Luke 20:27-40

Now some of the Sadducees who say that there is no resurrection came to Him [28]and they questioned Him, saying, "Teacher, Moses wrote for us a law that if a man's brother dies, leaving a wife and no children, his brother should marry the wife and raise the children for his brother. [29]Now there were seven brothers; and the first took a wife and died childless. [30] And the second, [31]and the third married her, and in the same way all seven died, leaving no children. [32]Finally the woman also died. [33]So in the life after resurrection, whose wife does she become? For all seven had married her." [34]Jesus said to them, "The sons of this world and present age marry and the women are given in marriage; [35]but those who are considered worthy to gain that other world and that future age and the resurrection from the dead, neither marry nor are given in marriage; [36]and they cannot die again, because they are immortal like the angels. And they are children of God, being participants in the resurrection. [37]But as for the fact that the dead are raised from death, even Moses showed, in the *passage about the burning* bush, when he calls the Lord the God of Abraham, the God of Isaac, and the God of Jacob. [38]Now He is not the God of the dead, but of the living so these forefathers will be among the resurrected; for all live in a definite relationship to Him." [39]Some of the scribes replied, "Teacher, you have spoken well so that there is no room for blame." [40]And they did not dare to question Him further about anything because of the wisdom He displayed in His answers.

☐ ☐ ☐ ☐ ☐ ☐ ☐ ☐ (32)

Risen Saviour, I give You thanks that I am marked in You with the seal of Your promised Holy Spirit, who is the Deposit guaranteeing my inheritance, as a child of Your resurrection and redemption.[246] I thank You, Jesus Christ, that You have indeed been raised from the dead, the first fruits of those who have fallen asleep.[247] I know that death has been swallowed up by Your victory.[248] I gratefuly stand firm in my identification with this victory. I give myself fully to Your work because I know that my labour in You, and for You, is not in vain.[249] I praise You as my living

---

[246] Ephesians 1:13, 14

[247] 1 Corinthians 15:20

[248] 1 Corinthians 15:54

God. I want to live as a person alive to You, fully alive in Christ, so help me God.

I need You to teach me day by day, according to each day's unfolding opportunities and needs. Give me, O my Lord, that purity of conscience to receive and to improve my apprehension of Your inspiration in my life. It seems my ears are so dull, I cannot hear Your voice as quickly and clearly as I ought and my eyes are dim such that I can not see You as I want. You alone can enhance my hearing, focus my sight; please cleanse and renew my heart. Teach me to sit at Your feet.[250]

O Lord in whose boundless being are laid up all treasures of wisdom, truth and holiness, grant to me through my constant fellowship with You the graces of Christian character. May these more and more take shape within my soul. May the grace of a thankful and an uncomplaining heart, the grace to await You with patience and to answer Your call promptly be given to me. May these virtues be sewn into my character. May the grace of courage, whether in suffering or in danger, the grace to endure hardness as an obedient apprentice of Jesus Christ, and the grace of boldness to stand for what is right be granted to me. May the grace of preparedness, the grace of bodily discipline, and the grace of strict truthfulness be features of my increasing Christ-likeness. Dear Lord, may the grace to treat others as I would have others treat me and as they themselves would like to be treated be seen in me. May the grace of authentic love, that refrains from hasty judgment, the grace of silence, that refrains from hasty speech and the grace of forgiveness towards all who have wronged me become etched into the way I habitually live out the Christ-life.

Heavenly Father, I commend to Your mercy the sick in body and mind. Have mercy on the elderly who are confined to their residences.[251] I call upon You, as Master, to be my helper and protector. Save the afflicted among us; have mercy on the lowly; raise up the fallen; appear to the needy; heal the ungodly; restore the wanderers; feed the hungry; ransom prisoners; raise up the sick; and comfort the faint-hearted.[252]

This is the world You love so much. You gave Your only begotten Son, my Lord and Saviour Jesus Christ, to hang from the Cross because of this love. Love was nearly

---

[249] 1 Corinthians 15:56-58

[250] Adapted from John Henry Newman

[251] John R. W. Stott

[252] Clement of Rome, 1st century

overwhelmed by hate, light nearly extinguished by darkness, and life nearly destroyed by His death. But love vanquished hate. For life overcame death and light overwhelmed darkness so now I can live with hope. The Lord Jesus Christ died BUT He was raised from the dead. He is risen. O my God, our God, O my Father when will I ever learn? When will they ever learn?[253]

Merciful Lord and Saviour, may the grace of tenderness towards all who are weaker than myself and the grace of steadfastness in continuing to desire that Your will be done and be evident in my life. And now, O God, give me a quiet mind, as I lie down to rest. Dwell in my thoughts until sleep overtakes me. Let me rejoice in the knowledge that, whether awake or asleep, You are still and ever with me. Let no troubling dreams disturb me. Awaken me, refreshed and ready for the tasks of another day.[254] I thank You for the resurrection power that is mine through Jesus as I engage a new day tomorrow, in Your Name.

---

[253] Desmond Tutu

[254] Adapted from John Baillie, 1949

Gospel Reading: Luke 20:41-21:4

Then He said to them, "How *is it that* people say that the Christ, the Messiah, the Anointed, is David's son? [42]For David himself says in the book of Psalms, 'The Father said to the Son, the Messiah, "Sit at My right hand, [43]Unil I make Your enemies a footstool for Your feet."' [44]So David calls the Son 'Lord,' and how *then* is He David's son?" [45]And with all the people listening, He said to His disciples, [46]"Beware of the scribes, who like to walk around in long robes, displaying their prominence, and love respectful greetings in the crowded market places, and chief seats in the synagogues and places of honor at banquets. [47]These men who confiscate *and* devour widows' houses, and for a pretense offer long prayers. These men will receive the greater sentence of condemnation." Looking up, He saw the rich people putting their gifts into the treasury. [2]And He saw a poor widow putting in two small copper coins. [3]He said, "Truly I say to you, this poor widow has put in proportionally more than all *of them*; [4]for they all put in gifts from their abundance; but she out of her poverty put in all she had to live on.

 (33)

Lord Jesus, though You were rich, for my sake, You became poor, so that through Your poverty I might become rich.[255] I am reminded tonight that whoever sows sparingly will also reap sparingly and whoever sows generously will also reap generously.[256] Lord may I be a generous, unpretentious, thankful, cheerful giver rather than a taker. Help me to share from what I have been given in sacrificial ways and with an eagerness to be useful to You and to those in need. Thank You for the grace of giving and for the gift of personal humility that triggers Your grace in my life.

Fix my steps, O Lord, so I don't stagger at the uneven motions of the world, but give me a steadiness to walk, full of Your Spirit and in a manner worthy of my calling.[257] O Father, I praise You that You understand my every sorrow and tear. I acknowledge my insufficiency to handle life's problems in my own strength. I gladly acknowledge my dependence upon You. May Your

---

[255] 2 Corinthians 8:9

[256] 2 Corinthians 9:6

[257] Adapted from John Wesley

grace abound to meet my deepest needs. Sustain me as I wait upon You. Fill my heart with Your peace that passes all understanding. Thank You for Your rich provision for me this day, in the Name of our Lord Jesus Christ. Amen.[258]

I falter where I have once firmly walked. God, I stretch my lame hand of faith to take hold of You. Eternal God, You have been the hope and joy of many generations, and in all ages You have given all people the power to seek You. In seeking to find You, grant me a clearer vision of Your truth, a greater faith in Your power, and a more confident assurance of Your love. When the way seems dark before me, give me grace to walk trustingly. When much is obscure to me, let me be all the more wide-awake to the little that I can clearly see. When the distant scene is clouded, let me rejoice that at least the next step is plain. When You are hidden from my eyes, let me still hold fast to what You command. When insight falters, let obedience stand firm. What I lack in faith let me repay in love. O infinite God, the brightness of whose face is often shrouded from my mortal gaze, I thank You that You sent Your Son Jesus Christ to be the light for this dark world. O Christ, You are Light of

light. I thank You that in Your most holy life You pierced the eternal mystery as with a great shaft of heavenly light; so that in seeing You I see Him whom no person has seen at any time. O my holy God I confess my sins before You and seek Your pardon in Jesus Christ my Lord. Amen.[259]

O merciful God, fill my heart. I pray, with the graces of Your Holy Spirit: love, joy, peace, patience, gentleness, goodness, faithfulness, humility and self-control. Teach me to love those who hate me; to pray for those who despitefully use me; that I may be a child of Your love. My Father, You make the sun to rise on the evil and the good, and send rain to fall on the just and on the unjust. In adversity grant me grace to be patient and in prosperity keep me humble. May I guard the door of my lips; may I lightly esteem the pleasures of this world, and may I thirst after heavenly things, through Jesus Christ my Lord.[260]

O God, enlarge within me the sense of fellowship with all living things, my brothers the animals to whom You gave the earth as their home in common with me. I remember with shame that we, as humans, have exercised high dominion with ruthless cruelty so that

---

[258] Luis Palau

[259] Adapted from John Baillie, 1949

[260] Anselm, 1033-1109

the voice of the earth, which should
have gone up to You in song, has
become a groan of travail. May I
realize that these live not for us alone
but for themselves and for You, and
that they too love the sweetness of life.[261]

Lord, You seized me and I could
not resist You; You overtook me; I
struggled; and You won. Here I am,
Lord, out of breath, out of day, no
fight left in me, and I've said YES,
almost unwillingly. Your look of love
has fallen on me. I am beginning to
understand You without hearing You.
I desire only You.[262] I love You Lord
Jesus Christ. Be with me through the
night.

[261] Basil the Great, c.330-379

[262] Michel Quoist (Prayers of Life)

Gospel Reading: Luke 21:5-19

As some were talking about the temple, that it was decorated with beautiful stones and consecrated offerings of magnificent gifts of gold which were displayed on the walls and hung in the porticoes, He said, [6]"As for all these things which you see, the time will come when there will not be one stone left on another that will not be torn down." [7]They asked Him, "Teacher, when will these things happen? And what will be the sign when these things are about to happen?" [8]He said, "Be careful *and* see to it that you are not misled; for many will come in My name, saying, 'I am *He*,' and, 'The time is near!' Do not follow them. [9]When you hear of wars, disturbances, civil unrest, revolts, and uprisings, do not panic; for these things must take place first, but the end will not *come* immediately." [10]Then Jesus told them, "Nation will rise against nation and kingdom against kingdom. [11]There will be violent earthquakes, and in various places famines and deadly and devastating plagues and epidemics; and there will be terrible sights and great signs from heaven. [12]"But before all these things, they will lay their hands on you and will persecute you, turning you over to the synagogues and prisons, and bringing you before kings and governors for My name's sake. [13]This will be a time *and* an opportunity for you to testify about Me. [14]So make up your minds not to prepare beforehand to defend yourselves; [15]for I will give you skillful words and wisdom which none of your opponents will be able to resist or refute. [16]But you will be betrayed *and* handed over even by parents and brothers and relatives and friends, and they will put *some* of you to death, [17]and you will be *continually* hated by everyone because of your association with My name. [18]But not a hair of your head will perish. [19]By your patient endurance, empowered by the Holy Spirit, you will gain your souls.

☐ ☐ ☐ ☐ ☐ ☐ ☐ ☐ (34)

O Triune God, my foundation and the rock of my salvation, I earnestly desire to stand firm and to gain life. I determine to receive and use Your Words and wisdom from above to live in obedience to the high calling I have received as a servant of the King of kings. May my body, Your temple, be put to good use. Displace my worries and disabling habits with an adaptive confidence in Your protective and compassionate ways. Equip me this week for whatever will come as challenges to my life. Root me deeply in Your patterns of thinking, doing, daring and being. Ready me for what is to come. Still my heart, solidify my disciplines of heart, mind and body for sustained well-being. Be my teacher, my advocate, and my companion along the way. I love You. I need You. I worship You.

LORD, I cry to You, make haste give ear to my voice when I cry to You. Let my prayer be set forth before You as incense; and the lifting up of my hands as the evening sacrifice. O Lord, open my lips, and my mouth shall show forth Your praise. Bless the Lord, O my soul, and let me not forget all Your benefits. You have forgiven all my iniquities. You have healed all my diseases. You have redeemed my life from destruction. You, O Lord, have crowned me with lovingkindness and tender mercies. You have satisfied my mouth with good things; so that I have been renewed. Cleanse me from secret faults.

Keep back Your servant from presumptuous sins; let these not have dominion over me. Then shall I be upright and be innocent from small and great transgressions. Have mercy upon me, O God, according to Your lovingkindness and according to the multitude of Your tender mercies, blot out my transgressions. Wash me thoroughly from my iniquity, and cleanse me from my sin. For I acknowledge my transgressions: and my sin is ever before me. Be my strong habitation, You are the One who I come running to. So will I sing praise to Your Name for ever. You, Lord, make me dwell in safety. Amen.[263]

O God, King of Righteousness, lead me, I pray to You, in the ways of justice and of peace. Lord inspire me to break down all tyranny and to gain for every person their due reward.[264] Heavenly Father, may Your Holy Spirit lead the rich nations to support the poor, and the strong nations to protect the weak; so that every nation may work together with other nations in true partnership for the promotion of peace and the good of all humankind, through Jesus Christ my Lord.[265]

God of all goodness, grant me the ardent desire to seek wisely, to know surely, and to accomplish perfectly Your holy will.[266] O God, Your Word tells me that, whatever my hand finds to do, I must do it with all my might. Help me as I prepare for tomorrow to concentrate with my whole attention on whatever I am doing and to keep

[263] Adapted from John Baillie, 1949
[264] William Temple, 1881-1944
[265] Source unknown
[266] Saint Thomas Aquinas

my thoughts from wandering. When I am studying, help me to study with my whole mind. When I am playing, help me to play with my whole heart. Help me to do one thing at a time, and to do it well. This capacity to be a focused person I ask for Jesus' sake.[267]

Father, after this night there will be a new day. I take it as a present from You. I want to arrive at the end of it knowing that You are pleased because I have enjoyed it properly and haven't neglected it, broken it, misused it, abused it, wasted it or, in any way, spoiled this gift. So I ask that I may be filled with Your Spirit right now and that, being filled with Your love, I may love the Lord Jesus Christ with the same love as is in You. May I serve You Jesus by washing the feet of Your disciples and by blessing my neighbours. In His name, Amen.[268] Oh, how I love You Jesus. Oh, how I love You Jesus. Oh, how I love You Jesus, because You first loved me.[269]

[267] William Barclay

[268] Roger Forster

[269] Frederick Whitfield

Gospel Reading: Luke 21:20-28

"But when you see Jerusalem surrounded by hostile armies, then understand with confident assurance that her complete destruction is near. [21]At that time, those who are in Judea must flee to the mountains, and those who are inside the city of Jerusalem must get out, and those who are out in the country must not enter the city; [22]for these are days of vengeance of rendering full justice or satisfaction, so that all things which are written will be fulfilled. [23]Woe to those women who are pregnant and to those who are nursing babies in those days! For great trouble *and* anguish will be on the land, and wrath *and* retribution on Israel. [24]And they will fall by the edge of the sword, and will be led captive into all nations; and Jerusalem will be trampled underfoot by the Gentiles until the times of the Gentiles are fulfilled. [25]"There will be signs attesting to miracles in the sun and moon and stars; and on the earth there will be distress *and* anguish among nations, in perplexity at the roaring *and* tossing of the sea and the waves, [26]people fainting from fear and expectation of the dreadful things coming on the world; for the very powers of the heavens will be shaken. [27]Then they will see the Son of Man coming in a cloud with transcendent and overwhelming power to subdue the nations, with great glory. [28]Now when these things begin to occur, stand tall and lift up your heads in joy, because suffering ends as your redemption is drawing near.

 (35)

To be wide-awake to these times it is fairly easy to see desolation, exodus of refugees, dreadful circumstances for mothers, children and families, great distress amongs nations, groaning lands and waters, anxiety and perplexity. On the news, I see with some fainting from terror, shaking with apprehension and suffering from their being trampled, exploited and held captive to injustice and evil. And just as the weight and burden of being surrounded on all sides by these conditions draws my eyes to my feet and the ground, may Your Spirit, the Spirit of Light and Truth draw my eyes heavenward in enthusiastic expectation of Your coming again and inspire my hope in Your sovereign and loving safekeeping of those who love You and are called by Your Name. Oh God help us in these difficult times!

God of mercy, You care for me as if there was no one else to care for.

I commend to You my own needs but also the needs of all this world. Remember me in Your mercy, O God, and keep me by Your grace. Forgive the scanty use I have made today of the talents You have entrusted to my keeping. Cover for the poverty of my service by the fullness of Your own divine resource. Grant also that, as day succeeds day, that I may be so strengthened by Your help that my service grows more worthy and my sins less grievous. May Christ more and more reign in my heart and purify my deeds. O God, remember in Your mercy all Your children. Let the whole earth be filled with Your praise and be made glad by the knowledge of Your Name.

Let there fall upon all humankind a sense of Your excellent greatness. Let the nations fear You. Let Your glory rule over every court and in their market-place. Let Your law be honoured in every home. Redeem the whole world's life, O God, and transform it utterly through the power of Your Holy Cross. I pray for all who devote their lives to the evangelization in and of the world. I pray for all international workers. I pray for those whose market place witness and use of resources bring honour to You. I pray for all those who are working in the cause of peace and understanding between the nations, and for all who are striving to break down the dividing walls between Jew and Gentile, bond and free, and make efforts to make all one in Christ Jesus. Encourage them with the joy of Your presence; and kindle in me the urgent desire to further support their labours as far as in me lies possible, through Jesus Christ. Amen.[270]

Almighty God, You are the giver of all good things, without whose help all labour is ineffectual, and without whose grace all wisdom would be folly. Grant, that, in all my undertakings, Your Holy Spirit may not be withheld from me but that I may promote Your glory. Grant this, O Lord, for the sake of Jesus Christ my Lord.[271] If tomorrow I should get lost amid the perplexities of life and the rush of many duties, search me out, gracious Lord, and bring me back into the quiet of Your presence.[272]

O Lord Jesus Christ, You who at the carpenter's bench manifest the dignity of honest labour, and gave to each of us tasks to perform, help me to do my work with readiness of mind and singleness of heart. May my service not be mere performance-for-appearance-sake as found with

---

[270] Adapted from John Baillie, 1949

[271] Samuel Johnson, 1709-84

[272] F. B. Meyer

common people-pleasers, but my I act as Your servant, labouring heartily as unto You. Whatever I do, great or small, it may be to the glory of Your Holy Name.[273] Keep me in Your love so that my love for You is kept and expressed through the night and day. May everything be directed to Your glory. May I never despair, for I am under Your hand and in You is all power and goodness.[274]

God, send revival that will turn the people of God back from their worldliness and idols to serve the true and living God. Keep me from relying on broken cisterns and turn me to rely on the Fountain of Living Waters. You, Yourself, are the source of all refreshment. Save the people of God from covetousness and the love of the world, and from all uncleanness of spirit, mind and body. Yes! Send a revival that will never need to be revived! But will sweep upon us like a mighty wave of the sea such that nothing can hinder, until time shall be no more! For such a sustained revival, O God, I pray.[275]

---

[273] John R. W. Stott

[274] Dag Hannarskjold

[275] A Prayer for Revival (part two)

Gospel Reading: Luke 21:29-38

Then He told them a parable: "Look at the fig tree and all the trees; [30]as soon as they put out leaves, you see it and know for yourselves that summer is near. [31]So you too, when you see these things happening, know without any doubt that the kingdom of God is near. [32]I assure you *and* most solemnly say to you, those living at that definite period of time preceding the second coming will not pass away until everything takes place. [33]Heaven and earth will pass away, but My words will not pass away. [34]"But be on guard, so that your hearts are not weighed down *and* depressed with the giddiness of debauchery and the nausea of self-indulgence and the worldly worries of life, and then that day when the Messiah returns will not come on you suddenly like a trap; [35]for it will come upon all those who live on the face of all the earth. [36]But keep alert at all times be attentive and ready, praying that you may have the strength *and* ability to be found worthy and to escape all these things that are going to take place, and to stand in the presence of the Son of Man at His coming." [37]Now in the daytime Jesus was teaching in the porches and courts of the temple, but at night He would go out and spend the night on the mount that is called Olivet. [38]And early in the morning all the people would come to Him in the temple to listen to Him.

 (36)

I come this evening in the strong name of Him who said: *If you continue in My Word, you shall know the truth, and the truth shall make you free.* I thank You for my family, good health, good friends, and all the things I so often take for granted. I thank You for the keen challenges of this past day, for work to do that demands the best I have to offer and still finds me inadequate. Tonight I seek Your help, knowing that in partnership with You there will be no dull moments and no problems beyond solution. God bless me and help me to be right in my thinking, good in my acting and virtuous in my deciding. I come in prayer to You, Lord Jesus, who never had to take back anything spoken, to correct anything said, nor apologize for any statement. Will You have mercy on my frailties and deliver me from being downcast? Teach me how to relax, to rest well and to make time to turn to You for guidance and for grace. In Your name I ask. Amen.[276]

---

[276] Adapted from Peter Marshall (1902–67)

O God of peace, unite my heart with others by Your bond of peace, that those I live and work with may live with one another continually in gentleness and humility, in peace and unity. O God of patience, give me patience in the time of trial, and steadfastness to endure to the end. O spirit of prayer, awaken my heart, that I may lift up holy hands to God, and cry to You in all my distresses. O gentle wind, cool and refresh my heart in all heat and anguish. Be my defence and shade in the time of need, my help in trial, my consolation when all things are against me. Come, O Eternal Light, Salvation, Comfort, be my light in darkness, my salvation in life, my comfort in death; and lead me in the straight way to everlasting life, that I may praise You, forever.[277]

Your kingdom come on earth as it is in heaven, O Lord. As I stand to watch and to pray, I do so in anticipation of Your working in and through me, together with Your intervention in the affairs of humankind. Thank You that You became flesh and dwelt amongst us. Thank You that the Son of God became the Son of man that the sons and daughters of men and women might become the children of God. May many from all tongues, tribes and geographies receive You into their lives and know the adoption experience of our loving God.

O Lord my God, again I thank You for bringing this day to a close. Thank You for giving me rest in body and soul. Your hand has been over me and You have guarded and preserved me. Forgive my lack of faith and any wrong that I have done today, and help me to forgive all who have wronged me. Let me sleep in peace under Your protection, and keep me from all the temptations of darkness. Into Your hands I commend my loved ones and all who dwell in this house. I commend to You my body and soul. O God, Your holy Name be praised.[278] May You, Lord Jesus Christ, be near to defend me, within to refresh me, around to preserve me, before to guide me, behind to justify me, and above to bless me. You, my Lord, live and reign with the Father and the Holy Spirit, for evermore.[279]

Grant to me, O Lord, to know that which is worth knowing, to love that which is worth loving, to praise that which can bear with praise, to hate what in Your sight is unworthy, to prize what to You is precious, and above all to search out and to do what

[277] Bernhard Albrecht, 1569-1636

[278] Dietrich Bonhoeffer
[279] Source unknown

is well-pleasing to You, through Jesus Christ my Lord. Amen.[280]

O Trinity, uncreated and without beginning, O undivided Unity, three and one, Father, Son and Spirit, a single God, accept this my hymn from tongue of clay.[281] Almighty and everlasting God, Comfort of the sad and Strength of sufferers, let the prayers of those who cry out come to You, that all may rejoice to find that Your mercy is present with those in affliction, through Jesus Christ my Lord. Amen.[282]

Into the night I go with the knowledge and comfort of Your abiding love. I love You Lord.

---

[280] Thomas A Kempis

[281] Lenten Triodiop

[282] Gelasian Sacramentary

Gospel Reading: Luke 22:1-13

Then He told them a parable: "Look at the fig tree and all the trees; [30]as soon as they put out leaves, you see it and know for yourselves that summer is near. [31]So you too, when you see these things happening, know without any doubt that the kingdom of God is near. [32]I assure you *and* most solemnly say to you, those living at that definite period of time preceding the second coming will not pass away until everything takes place. [33]Heaven and earth will pass away, but My words will not pass away. [34]"But be on guard, so that your hearts are not weighed down *and* depressed with the giddiness of debauchery and the nausea of self-indulgence and the worldly worries of life, and then that day when the Messiah returns will not come on you suddenly like a trap; [35]for it will come upon all those who live on the face of all the earth. [36]But keep alert at all times be attentive and ready, praying that you may have the strength *and* ability to be found worthy and to escape all these things that are going to take place, and to stand in the presence of the Son of Man at His coming." [37]Now in the daytime Jesus was teaching in the porches and courts of the temple, but at night He would go out and spend the night on the mount that is called Olivet. [38]And early in the morning all the people would come to Him in the temple to listen to Him.

 (37)

I believe in the downfall and defeat of Satan and his cohorts. With this prayer, I pledge my allegiance to the Lord Jesus Christ and separate myself completely and unreservedly from the father of lies and prince of darkness. I take on the armour of God. I know I am strong in the Lord and His mighty power. In Jesus' Name I take my stand against the evil one and his schemes. I wear the belt of Your truth, O God. I wear the breastplate of Your righteousness and fit my feet with the readiness of the Gospel of Peace. The shield of faith will extinguish the flaming arrows, aimed by the evil one at my family and others I dearly love. I take the helmet of salvation and the sword of the Spirit, Your eternal Word. Teach me, O Lord, to pray in the Spirit on all occasions with all kinds of prayers and requests to be alert and to make know the mysteries of Your Gospel.[283]

You my God are the only origin of all that is good, fair, and true. To

---

[283] Galatians 6:10-20

You alone I lift up my soul. O God, let Your Spirit fill my heart. I pray this prayer with all that is in me and from the deep parts of my soul. O God, give me power to follow after that which is good. Let there be no secret purpose of evil formed in my mind, that waits for an opportunity of fulfilment. O God, bless all my undertakings and cause these to prosper. Now as I pray this prayer, let me not hold onto any undertakings for which I have not asked Your blessing. God, bless every member of my home and family. As I pray this prayer, let me not harbour in my heart a wrongful feeling of jealousy or bitterness or anger towards any of them. God, bless my enemies and those who have done me wrong. God, let Your Kingdom come on earth. Let me not devote my best hours and years to the service of lesser ends. O Holy Spirit of God, as I rise from these acts of devotion, let me not return to evil thoughts or worldly ways, but let that mind be in me which was also in Jesus. Amen.[284]

Lord help me to prepare my heart to fellowship with You – sleeping or awake. I want to be with You. I want to be fiercely loyal to You and Your Kingdom. Regardless of the devices and desires of the wicked, I will trust,

obey and love You with all my heart, so help me Lord.

Lord, I pray for Your people. May Your eyes may be upon them day and night. Tenderly spread Your care to protect them. Stretch forth Your holy right hand to bless them. Pour into their hearts Your Holy Spirit to abide with them, to refresh them with devotion, to stimulate them with hope, and to inflame them with love. Kind Consoler, help them in temptation and strengthen them in all the tribulations of this life.[285]

As I prepare to get a good night's sleep so that I can go into the world in peace, I wish to be of good courage to hold fast to that which is good, to strengthen the faint hearted, to support the weak, to help the afflicted, to honour all persons, to love and serve the Lord, and to rejoice in the power of the Holy Spirit. And so may the blessing of God Almighty, the Father, the Son, and the Holy Ghost, be upon me, and remain with me for ever.[286] To You, O God, I give myself entirely all the days of my life. I give You my understandings, my will, and my affections. Lord, what You love may I also love; what You hate may I hate. May I glorify You with my body; preserving it fit for You to dwell in. I

[284] Adapted from John Baillie, 1949

[285] Aelred, 1109-1167

[286] Church of England. Book of Common Prayer (with the Additions and Deviations Proposed in 1928)

give You myself, my reputation and my all. Be my portion and my all. O God, when foolishly tempted to break this solemn engagement with You, may my answer be: *I am not my own but I belong entirely to God.* God be merciful to me, a sinner. Amen.[287]

Almighty God, Holy Spirit, who proceeds from the Father and the Son, kindle in me the true knowledge and love of God. Stir up in my heart true fear, true faith, and acknowledgement of the mercy promised to me. Be my comforter in all difficulties and dangers, and so kindle divine love in my heart, that by true obedience I may offer perpetual praise to You Father, to Your redeeming Son, and to Your blessed Holy Spirit. Amen.[288]

---

[287] John Wesley

[288] Philip Melancthon

Gospel Reading: Luke 22:14-30

When the hour for the meal had come, Jesus reclined *at the table*, and the apostles with Him. [15]He said to them, "I have earnestly wanted to eat this Passover with you before I suffer; [16]for I say to you, I will not eat it again until it is fulfilled in the kingdom of God." [17]And when He had taken a cup and given thanks, He said, "Take this and share it among yourselves; [18]for I say to you, I will not drink of the fruit of the vine from now on until the kingdom of God comes." [19]And when He had taken bread and given thanks, He broke it and gave it to them, saying, "This is My body which is given for you; do this in remembrance of Me." [20]And in the same way *He took* the cup after they had eaten, saying, "This cup, which is poured out for you, is the new covenant ratified in My blood. [21]But listen, the hand of the one betraying Me is with Mine on the table. [22]For indeed, the Son of Man is going as it has been determined; but judgment is coming to that man by whom He is betrayed *and* handed over!" [23]And they began to discuss among themselves which one of them it might be who was going to do this. [24]Now a dispute also arose among them as to which of them was regarded to be the greatest. [25]Jesus said to them, "The kings of the Gentiles have absolute power *and* lord it over them; and those in authority over them are called 'Benefactors.' [26]But it is not to be this way with you; on the contrary, the one who is the greatest among you must become like the youngest and least privileged, and the one who is the leader, like the servant. [27]For who is the greater, the one who reclines *at the table* or the one who serves? Is it not the one who reclines *at the table*? But I am among you as the one who serves. [28]"You are those who have remained *and* have stood by Me in My trials; [29]and just as My Father has granted Me a kingdom, I grant you the privilege [30]that you may eat and drink at My table in My kingdom, and you will sit on thrones judging the twelve tribes of Israel.

☐ ☐ ☐ ☐ ☐ ☐ ☐ ☐ (38)

This evening I remember with profound gratitude Your broken body and Your shed blood, Lord Jesus Christ. I recall Your suffering for me. I thank You for the love that constained You to give up Your life – the perfectly lived life – for me. Your death was an atonement for my sins. It was the Cross I deserved but You substituted for me. I give You thanks for my deliverance from sin, death and the evil one. I desire to be a servant in Your kingdom. May Your kingdom come on earth as it is in heaven. I seek first Your kingdom and Your righteousness. I love You Lord Jesus.

O Lord my God, in the face of life's mysteries and its vast imponderables, give me faith to believe that You make all things to work together for good to those who love You and are called to Your purposes. Strengthen my conviction that Your hand is upon me, to lead me and to use me in working out Your purposes in the world. Even though I may not see the distant scene, let me be willing to take one step at a time and trust You for the rest. O Father God, my trust is in You. You alone know the end from the beginning, and I must walk by faith. I am anxious about the consequences of what I've done today and will do tomorrow. May that concern both restrain and inspire me in my private life as it does in my public duty. Translate all my works into Your purposes and be honoured and glorified by my behaviour, O God. In my troubled mind there is confusion and honest perplexity, but I know there is no confusion with You. Please guide me, that I may do what it is I ought to do and leave undone those things that I need to leave alone. This I ask in Christ's Name, the same Christ who was crucified, having done nothing amiss. Amen.[289]

O God, bless to me each thing my eye sees. O God, bless to me each sound that comes to me. O God, bless to me each savour that I smell. O God, bless to me each taste dwelling in my mouth; each ray that guides my way, each thing that I pursue, and the zeal that seeks my living soul.[290] I go into the night to sleep in peace; the wisdom of the Wonderful Counsellor guides me, the strength of the Mighty God defends me, the love of the Everlasting Father enfolds me, and the peace of the Prince of Peace is upon me. I know that the blessing of God Almighty, Father, Son, and Holy Spirit is with me all this night and for evermore.[291] Keep me in peace, O Christ my God, under the protection of Your holy and venerable cross; save me from my enemies, visible and invisible, and count me worthy to glorify You with thanksgiving, with the Father and the Holy Spirit, now and for ever, world without end.[292]

To thank You properly is impossible. To thank You according to my ability is right and proper. For You have redeemed me from the waste of worshipping many gods and delivered

[289] Adapted from Peter Marshall (1902–67)

[290] Source unknown (Early Scottish)

[291] Source unknown

[292] Source unknown (Armenian Orthodox dismissal)

me from error and ignorance. You sent Christ as a human being among humans, Christ who is the only-begotten God. You have caused Your Holy Spirit to dwell in me. You have given Your angels charge over me. You have put the devil to shame. When I was not, You made me. You take care of me. You measure out life to me. You provide me with people to love, work to do and food to sustain me. You have promised redemption. For all these things, may glory and worship be to You through Jesus Christ, now, and for ever, and throughout all ages. Amen.[293]

Almighty God, give me the grace to cast away the works of darkness and to put on the armour of light. In the time of His mortal life Your Son, Jesus Christ, came to us in great humility. I know that the last day is coming, when He will come again in His glorious majesty to judge the living and the dead. May I may rise to the life immortal, through Him who is ever alive and who reigns with You, in the unity of the Holy Spirit, one God, now and forever.[294]

Praise to the Holiest in the height and in the depth be praise, in all His Words most wonderful, most sure in all His ways. O loving wisdom of our God, when all was sin and shame, a second Adam to the fight and to the rescue came. O generous love! Praise to the Holiest in the heights, and in the depth be praise; in all His Words most wonderful, most sure in all His ways.[295] Lord I love You.

[293] Apostolic Constitutions

[294] Reflections on Daily Prayer

[295] John Henry Newman (1801-1890)

Gospel Reading: Luke 22:31-38

"Simon, Simon Peter, listen! Satan has demanded permission to sift all of you like grain; [32]but I have prayed especially for you, Peter, that your faith and confidence in Me may not fail; and you, once you have turned back again to Me, strengthen and support your brothers in the faith." [33]And Peter said to Him, "Lord, I am ready to go with You both to prison and to death!" [34]Jesus said, "I say to you, Peter, before the rooster crows today, you will utterly deny three times that you know Me." [35]And He said to them, "When I sent you out without a money belt and provision bag and extra sandals, did you lack anything?" They answered, "Nothing." [36]Then He said to them, "But now, he who has a money belt is to take it along, and also his provision bag, and he who has no sword is to sell his coat and buy one. [37]For I tell you that this Scripture which is written must be completed and fulfilled in Me: 'and He was counted with the criminals'; for that which refers to Me has its fulfillment and is settled." [38]They said, "Lord, look, here are two swords." And He said to them, "It is enough.

 (39)

Jesus Christ You sit on the right hand of the Majesty on high, making intercession for me. Please pray that my faith in You will not fail and that out of my integrity of life and fervent living for You I might be an encouragement to others. Lord, I will do anything, give up anything, go anywhere and be whatever Your will is for me. Prosper the efforts of my head, heart and hands and help me to live as I ought to. I need You for this O Lord. Benefit me with Your prayers and Your presence, I pray.

Gracious God, I seek Your presence at the close of another day, I ask You to create a pool of heavenly peace within my heart as I lie down to sleep. Let all the day's excitements and anxieties now give place to a time of inward recollection, as I wait upon You and meditate upon Your love. Dear Father, tonight give me a deeper sense of gratitude to You for all Your mercies. Your goodness to me has been wonderful. At no moment of in day have I lacked Your gracious care. At no moment have I been called upon to stand alone in my own strength. When I was too busy with my petty concerns to remember You, You with a universe to govern were not too busy to remember me. O God, I am bitterly ashamed that I must continually be confessing to You my forgetfulness of You, the feebleness of my love for You, the fitfulness and listlessness of my desires. How many plain commandments of Yours have I this day disobeyed? How many little services of love have I withheld from You, O Christ?

Dear Lord, if at this evening hour I think only of myself and my own condition and my own day's doings and my day's record of service, then I can find no peace before I go to sleep, but only experience bitterness of spirit and a miserable despair. Therefore, O Father, let me think rather of You and rejoice that Your love is great enough to blot out all my sins. And, O Christ, Lamb of God, let me think of You, and lean upon Your heavenly righteousness, taking no pleasure in what I am before You but only in what You are for me and in my stead. And, O Holy Spirit, think within me and so move within my mind and will that as the days go by I may be more and more conformed to the righteousness of Jesus Christ my Lord, to whom be glory for ever. Amen.[296]

Almighty God, who in Your wisdom so ordered my earthly life that I must walk by faith and not by sight, grant me such faith in You that, amidst all things that pass my understanding, I may believe in Your fatherly care, and ever be strengthened by the assurance that underneath are the everlasting arms.[297]

Our Father in heaven, You know every secret of my heart--all that I fear, all that I hope, and all of which I am ashamed today -- in this moment of confession. As I look into my heart and mind, have mercy upon me and make me clean inside, that in all I do tomorrow may I behave with true courtesy and honour. Compel me to be just and honest in all my dealings. Let my motives be above suspicion. Let my word be my bond. Let me be kind in my criticism of others, and slow to judge, knowing that I myself must one day be judged. O God, slow me down, for I know that I live too fast. If I am going to burn myself out, may it be in causes worth dying for. With all of eternity before me, make me take time to live, time to get acquainted with You, time to enjoy Your blessings, and time to know others as I ought. Deliver me from wasting time and teach me how to use it wisely and well. I pray for renewal to come upon me.[298]

God give me light to guide me, courage to support me, and love to unite me, now and evermore.[299] Lord

[296] Adapted from John Baillie, 1949

[297] Source unknown

[298] Adapted from Peter Marshall (1902–67)

bless and protect me. Lord smile on
me and show me Your favour. Lord
befriend me and prosper me.[300] May
the love of the Father enfold me; the
wisdom of the Son enlighten me; the
fire of the Spirit inflame me; and may
the blessing of the triune God rest
upon me, and abide with me, now and
evermore.[301] Let Your mighty hand, O
Lord God, and outstretched arm be my
defence; let Your mercy and lovingkindness in Jesus Christ, Your dear
Son, be my salvation. Let Your all-
true Word, be my instruction; and let
the grace of the lifegiving Spirit, be
my comfort and my consolation, to the
end and in the end.[302]

---

[299] Source unknown

[300] Source unknown

[301] Source unknown

[302] Church of Scotland. Book of Common Order

Gospel Reading: Luke 22:39-46

And He came out and went, as was His habit, to the Mount of Olives; and the disciples followed Him. [40]When He arrived at the place called Gethsemane, He said to them, "Pray *continually* that you may not fall into temptation." [41]And He withdrew from them about a stone's throw, and knelt down and prayed, [42]saying, "Father, if You are willing, remove this cup of divine wrath from Me; yet not My will, but always Yours be done." [43]Now an angel appeared to Him from heaven, strengthening Him. [44]And deeply distressed and anguished; almost to the point of death, He prayed more intently; and His sweat became like drops of blood, falling down on the ground. [45]When He rose from prayer, He came to the disciples and found them sleeping from sorrow, [46]and He said to them, "Why are you sleeping? Get up and pray that you may not fall into temptation.

 (40)

Our Father, in the midst of the complicated situations of life and the unsolved problems of the world, deliver Your servant from any sense of futility. Cause me to understand that Your power is never obstructed by difficulties, nor is Your love limited by the confusion or interruption of human plans. May the very failure of humankind's best resources to resolve messy problems impel me toward the infinite resources of God. Cleanse my heart of selfishness. Grant that all the critical questions before me be made clear. Forgive me, O God, for all my boasting and my presumptuous sins of pride and arrogance, for these are days that ought to humble me. By Your grace, I am becoming more and more aware of my limitations and my weaknesses. Help me to understand that with the proud and the self-sufficient You can do nothing. I need Your help to live this life, my Father, and I humbly seek this help. I want to do right, and to be right; so start me in the right way through this night sleep. O Lord, in the morning may I say, *I can do all things through Christ Who strengthens me.*[303]

God of mercy and grace, I pray that I will not fall into temptation and sin. I know that You are faithful and will not allow me to be tempted beyond what I can bear. Please provide a way out or a means to stand

[303] Adapted from Peter Marshall (1902–67)

up under temptations. Bring sensible people around me and remind me to wake up and pray – to express my ongoing dependence on You. I desparately need You to carry me through life. Strengthen me and provide whatever angelic assistance might be warranted.[304] I recall that You are my high priest, that You sympathize with my weaknesses and that You were tempted in every way – yet You did not sin. I approach Your throne of grace with confidence to receive mercy and grace in this my time of need.[305]

O Lord my God, You know my needs and the needs of those with whom I live and work. I am inadequate in my capacity to fulfill these needs. With Your help, O Lord, I will be infinitely better than I am, wiser than I know, and stronger than I could dream. In this prayer, I bring to You my family and co-workers, asking for Your blessing. Bestow upon each the courage to do right and be good even as You have given them the capacity to know the right, the good and the virtuous. Keep them well in all of their comings and goings, for Jesus' sake. Amen.[306]

O God, I am one with You. You have made me one with You. You have taught me that if I am open to others, You dwell amongst us. Help me to preserve this openness and to strive for it with all my heart. O God, in accepting one another wholeheartedly, fully, completely, I accept You. I thank you, I adore you, and I love you, with my whole being, because my spirit is rooted in Your Spirit. Fill me then with love and let me be bound in love with others as we go our diverse ways, united in You. Your love has overcome. Your love is victorious.[307]

Father, I pray for Your Church throughout the world, that She may share fully in the work of Your Son, revealing You to all Peoples and reconciling each person to You, and to one another. I pray that Christians may learn to love one another and their neighbours, as You have loved. I pray that Your Church may more and more reflect the unity which is Your will and Your gift. I pray through Jesus Christ my Lord.[308]

A mighty fortress is my God, a strong hold never failing; my Helper He amid the flood of mortal ills prevailing. For still my ancient foe conspires to work me woe; his craft

---

[304] 1 Corinthians 10:12-15

[305] Hebrews 4:15, 16

[306] Adapted from Peter Marshall (1902–67)

[307] Thomas Merton

[308] Coventry Cathedral (Prayer from the Chapel of Unity)

and power are great, and armed with bitter hate, on earth is not his equal. If I in my own strength confide, my strivings would be losing, unless God's man is on my side, the man of God's own choosing. They ask who that may be? Christ Jesus, it is He; the Lord of Hosts, His Name, from age to age the same, and He will win the battle.[309] I love You Lord Jesus.

---

[309] Martin Luther, 1529

Gospel Reading: Luke 22:47-62

While He was still speaking, a crowd *came*, and the man called Judas, one of the twelve disciples, was leading the way for them. He approached Jesus to kiss Him. ⁴⁸And Jesus said to him, "Judas, are you betraying the Son of Man with a kiss?" ⁴⁹When those who were around Him saw what was about to happen, they said, "Lord, should we strike with the sword?" ⁵⁰And one of them struck the slave of the high priest and cut off his right ear. ⁵¹But Jesus replied, "Stop! No more of this." And He touched the ear and healed him. ⁵²Then Jesus said to the chief priests and officers of the temple and elders of the Sanhedrin who had come out against Him, "Have you come out with swords and clubs as you would against a robber? ⁵³Day after day when I was with you in the temple, you did not lay hands on Me; but this hour and the power *and* authority of darkness are yours." ⁵⁴Then they seized Him, and led Him *away* and brought Him to the elegant house of the Jewish high priest. And Peter was following at a safe distance. ⁵⁵After they had kindled a fire in the middle of the courtyard and had sat down together, Peter sat among them. ⁵⁶And a servant-girl, seeing him as he sat in the firelight and looking intently at him, said, "This man was with Him too." ⁵⁷But Peter denied it, saying, "Woman, I do not know Him!" ⁵⁸A little later someone else saw him and said, "You are one of them too." But Peter said, "Man, I am not!" ⁵⁹After about an hour had passed, another man *began* to insist, "This man was with Him, for he is a Galilean too." ⁶⁰But Peter said, "Man, I do not know what you are talking about." Immediately, while he was still speaking, a rooster crowed. ⁶¹The Lord turned and looked at Peter. And Peter remembered the word of the Lord, how He had told him, "Before a rooster crows today, you will deny Me three times." ⁶²And he went out and wept, deeply grieved and distressed.

☐ ☐ ☐ ☐ ☐ ☐ ☐ ☐ (41)

Son of Man, Son of God, I give You thanks for Your accompaniment through this day. Tonight I express my concern that I may have given You only lip service and fained a superficial affiliation with You to others. I have not attended to Your voice nor depended on Your power at work in me as I ought to have done. I am sorry for this and want to turn from all passivity, betrayal, disownership or rote living. When it comes to You, I ought to live in vital relationship with You. I acknowledge that I can do nothing without You and that apart from You I am lost. Keep me close through this night and may I boldly declare in my living and with my lips the glory and boastings of God. May I be one with You and all who love You.

O most gracious God, let me now rejoice in the love You have shown to our poor human race. You have openned up to us a way whereby we might be delivered from our sin and foolishness. O God, I praise You for Your great and holy love. When I had utterly gone astray, You sought me out and saved me, sending Your well-beloved Son to suffer and to die that I might be restored to the fellowship of Your children. O God, I praise You for Your great and holy love. You humbled Yourself for my sake, consenting to share a common life in human form as 100 percent man; while never ceasing to be 100 percent God. You chose to dwell in the midst of all our sin and shame, to endure all the harshness of Your blessed Passion, and, at the last, to die upon the Cross. This that I might be released from my bondage and enter with You into the glorious liberty as a child of God. O God, I praise the great and holy love You daily shed abroad in my unworthy heart, the peace and joy of

sin forgiven, making me a partaker with all the saints. I rejoice in the blessings of my Lord's Incarnation, in Your passion and crucifixion, and in Your Resurrection and Ascension to the Father's right hand on high. O holy and blessed Trinity, let me now so dwell in the mystery of this heavenly love that all hatred and malice is rooted out from my heart and life. Let me love You, as You have first loved me; and in loving You let me love also my neighbour; and let me be saved from all false love of myself; and to You, Father, Son, and Holy Spirit, be all glory and praise for ever. Amen.[310]

O God the Father, You are good beyond all that is good and fair beyond all that is fair. In You there is calmness, peace, and concord. Please mend and make up the dissensions which divide us from each other, and may we bear some likeness to Your divine nature.[311] O Sovereign and almighty Lord, bless all Your people. May Your Church act as one body and with one spirit, in one hope of our calling, and benefit from Your divine and boundless love.[312]

Our Father, I acknowledge that You govern in the affairs of humankind. If a sparrow cannot fall to

---

[310] Adapted from John Baillie, 1949

[311] Liturgy of St Dionysius, 9th century

[312] Liturgy of St Mark, 2nd century

the ground without Your notice, how can I imagine You could be indifferent to what I say and do? If this week You want me to do, or not to do, any particular thing, I pray that You will make it plain to me. You know how blind and how stubborn I can be. I pray for Your help in my thinking and Your love in my heart. Before You, Lord, one day I shall give an account, please lend me Your aid, that this day's work may be well pleasing to You. Be courage in me, faith in me and may Your mind be my mind. Give life to my good intentions, so that the best of these are not still-born. Forgive my feverish ways. Reclothe me in my rightful mind, in purer life for Your service and in deeper reverence that may I ever praise You.

Take from my soul the strain and stress and let my ordered life confess the beauty of Your peace. Deliver me, O Lord from the foolishness of impatience. Let me not be in such a hurry as to run on without You. I know that it takes a lifetime to make a tree; I know that fruit does not ripen in an afternoon, and You Yourself took a week to make the universe. Slow me down, O Lord, that I may take time to think, time to pray, and time discern the unfolding plan in the outworking of Your will. Then give me the sense and the courage to do as I was made to do, for the glory of Your Name.

Amen.[313] Be with me through the night and into tomorrow Lord.

---

[313] Adapted from Peter Marshall (1902–67)

Gospel Reading: Luke 22:63-71

Now the men who were holding Jesus in custody were mocking *and* ridiculing Him, treating Him with contempt and beating Him. ⁶⁴They blindfolded Him and asked, "Prophesy, who is it that struck You?" ⁶⁵And they were saying many other evil and slanderous things against Him, speaking sacrilegiously and abusively about Him. ⁶⁶When day came, the Council of the elders of the people assembled, both chief priests and scribes; and they led Jesus away to the council *chamber*, saying, ⁶⁷"If You are the Christ, tell us." But He said to them, "If I tell you, you will not believe what I say, ⁶⁸and if I ask a question, you will not answer. ⁶⁹But from now on, the Son of Man will be seated at the right hand of the power of God." ⁷⁰And they all said, "Are You the Son of God, then?" He replied, "*It is just as* you say." ⁷¹Then they asked, "What further need of testimony do we have? For we ourselves have heard it from His own mouth.

 (42)

O Christ, Son of Man and Son of God, I worship You tonight, as I stand in Your presence and as You are seated at the right hand of the mighty Majesty. I find it torturous to recall that I once mocked and insulted You by my insolence, indifference and rebellion against You, my Creator. I was blind but now I see. I was a sinner when You expressed Your love to me and offered me the choice to repent, turn from my wicked ways, to receive Your forgiveness and to invite You to be my Lord and Saviour. I come again O Christ to worship You and to testify of my love for You. I remain a sinner but I have been redeemed and forgiven by Your blood. Hear my thanksgiving and my profound gratitude for Your amazing grace and love.

Father, hear the prayer I offer; not for ease that prayer shall be, but for strength that I may ever live my life courageously. Not forever in green pastures do I ask my way to be; but the steep and rugged pathway may I tread rejoicingly. Not for ever by still waters would I idly rest and stay; but would smite the living fountains from the rocks along the way. Be my strength in hours of weakness, in my wanderings be my guide; through endeavour, failure, danger, Father be at my side.³¹⁴

---

³¹⁴ Adapted from Love Maria Willis (1824-1908)

Your eternal love was most perfectly shown in Your life and death my Lord. Enable me now so to meditate upon Your passion that, having fellowship with You in Your sorrow, I may also learn the secret of Your strength and peace. I remember Gethsemane. I remember how Judas betrayed You. I remember how Peter denied You. I remember how they all forsook You and fled. I remember the scourging. I remember the crown of thorns. I remember how they spat upon You. I remember how they hit You on the head. I remember Your pierced hands and feet. I remember Your agony on the Cross. I remember Your thirst. I remember how You cried, *My God, my God, why have You forsaken me?* I may not know, I cannot tell, what pains You had to bear but I believe it was for me that You hung and suffered there. Grant, O most gracious God, that as I kneel before You that I may let the redeeming power that has flowed from Your sufferings through so many generations flow now into my soul. Here let me find forgiveness of sin. Here let me learn to share with You, my Christ, the burden of the suffering of the world. Amen.[315]

Help me to remember that they that wait upon the Lord shall renew their strength. May I wait and be made strong. I ask in the Name of Him who died for all, even Jesus Christ our Lord. Amen.[316] GOD disclose the brightness of Your presence and revive within me the hope of my faith. Deliver me from discouragement. Give me the boldness of a faith that has conviction as well as sentiment, and take from me all fear save that of failing to do Your will. Lord Jesus, I turn in confidence to You, since You were tempted in all points like I am, and yet You were without sin. I know that I am not what I ought to be; and I know that I am not yet what I will be; but I thank You that I am not what I once was.

For a clearer vision of the work You have set before me and for a better understanding of Your Gospel, *Lord, direct me.* For a deeper commitment in Your service and a greater love for all Your children, *Lord, direct me.* For a fresh understanding of the tasks before me and for a sense of urgency in my proclamation, *Lord, direct me.* For a greater respect and acceptance among Christians of different traditions and for a common goal in evangelism, *Lord, direct us.[317]* Lord of Light, shine on me. Lord of Peace, dwell in me. Lord of Might, undergird me. Lord of

[315] Adapted from John Baillie, 1949

[316] Adapted from Peter Marshall (1902–67)

[317] Anglican Province of the Indian Ocean

Love, enfold me. Lord of Wisdom,
enlighten me. Then, Lord, let me go
out as Your witnesses, in obedience to
Your command; to share the good
news of Your mighty love for me in
the gift of Your Son, my Saviour,
Jesus Christ.[318]

Give to Your Church, O God, a
bold vision and a daring love, a
refreshed wisdom and a courteous
understanding, that the eternal
message of Your Son may be
acclaimed and proclaimed as the Good
News of the Age, through Jesus Christ
my Lord.[319] As I sleep, ready me and
refresh me to glorify You in the
adventure of tomorrow. Oh, how I
love You. Amen.

---

[318] Church in Wales

[319] The Daily Office

Gospel Reading: Luke 23:1-12

Then the whole assembly got up and brought Him before Pilate. ²They began to accuse Jesus, asserting, "We found this Man misleading *and* perverting our nation and forbidding us to pay taxes to Caesar, and claiming that He Himself is the Messiah, the Anointed, a King." ³So Pilate asked Him, "Are You the King of the Jews?" And He answered him, "*It is just as* you say." ⁴Then Pilate said to the chief priests and the crowds, "I find no guilt in this Man." ⁵But they were insistent and said, "He stirs up the people to rebel, teaching throughout Judea, starting from Galilee even as far as here in Jerusalem." ⁶When Pilate heard it, he asked whether the man was a Galilean. ⁷And when he learned that He belonged to the jurisdiction of Herod Antipas, the tetrarch of Galilee, he sent Him to Herod, who was also in Jerusalem at that time. ⁸When Herod saw Jesus, he was exceedingly pleased. He had wanted to see Him for a long time because of what he had heard about Him, and was hoping to see some miraculous sign even something spectacular done by Him. ⁹And he questioned Him at some length, but Jesus made no reply. ¹⁰The chief priests and the scribes were standing there, *continually* accusing Him heatedly. ¹¹And Herod with his soldiers, after treating Him with contempt and mocking *and* ridiculing Him, dressed Him in a gorgeous robe and sent Him back to Pilate. ¹²Now that very day Herod and Pilate became friends with each other—before this they had been enemies.

 (43)

O King of the Jews, King of every tribe and every kin throughout the world, You are Lord of lords and King of kings. I worship You with a grateful heart and dedicate my life and work and all to You. I express my full dependence on You for the grace to deliver me from the power of sin and for every breath of life I breathe. You hold the world together by the power of Your Word; fill me afresh with Your Holy Spirit. I yield to Your wonder working in and through my life. May I overflow to the benefit of others, to the fulfillment of Your unique calling and purpose for my life and for Your kingdom sake. So help me God: Father, Son and Holy Spirit. I thank You Jesus that Your answer to me – as You see me with love – is "Yes!"

Give me open eyes to see the beauty all around me and to see it as Your handiwork. Let all lovely things fill me with gladness and let them lift up my heart in true worship. Give me this evening, O God, a strong and vivid sense that You are by my side. By Your grace, everywhere I go this week, please come. You have promised to give me the Holy Spirit if I am willing to open my heart and let You in. I know, deep down in my heart, that without Your guidance I can do nothing, but with You I can do all things. Let me not be frightened by the problems that confront me, but rather I give You thanks that You have matched me with this hour. May I resolve, Your helping me, to be part of the answer, and not part of the problem.[320]

Dear Lord and Father re-clothe me in my rightful mind, in a purer life, in deeper reverence and praise. Take from my soul the strain and stress, and let my ordered life confess the beauty of Your peace.[321] Father, Son and Holy Spirit, I yearn for a better understanding of spiritual things, so that I may know more surely what Your plan is for me and for all those I love and work with. Give to me a clear vision that I may know where to stand and what to stand for. Remind me, O God, that You have not resigned. Harassed and troubled by the difficulties and uncertainties that have

arisen this past week and in anticipation of more of the same tomorrow, I rest on You. As I rest in You, help me to set a pace that puts You first and foremost on my mind and in my heart. Deliver me, O God, from the God-helps-those-who-help-themselves philosophy, which can really be a cloak for my sheer unbelief in Your ability and willingness to take care of me and my affairs.

Tomorrow give to me a passion for what is in principle excellent, rather than that which is simply expedient, for what is morally right, just and virtuous, rather than socially or politically correct.[322] O clothe me with Your heavenly armour, Lord: Your trust and faith shield and Your sword of love divine. I ask no victories that are not Yours. Give or withhold, let pain or pleasure be enough to know that I am serving You.[323]

Eternal Father, make the Church of Your dear Son great and fair, the joy of the whole earth. Send Your Holy Spirit to direct me in all manner of wisdom, love, and might. Remove perplexity, establish concord, kindle the flame, and gather people who are of a strong faith to the praise of Him who with You and the Spirit live and reign, one God, world without end.[324]

[320] Adapted from Peter Marshall (1902–67)

[321] Adapted from Peter Marshall (1902–67)

[322] Adapted from Peter Marshall (1902–67)

[323] Adapted from John White Chadwick (1840-1904)

O God the Father of all, You ask every one to spread love where the poor are humiliated, joy where the Church is brought low, and reconciliation where people are divided.[325]

God You move in mysterious ways Your wonders to perform. You plant Your footsteps in the sea, and ride upon the storm. Your purposes will ripen fast, unfolding every hour; the bud may have a bitter taste, but sweet will be the flowers.[326] You've got the whole world in Your hand. You've got the whole world in Your hand. Yes, You've got the whole wide world in Your hand. You've got the whole world in Your hand.[327] Lord, tonight I place myself in Your care, in Your hands, for You care for me. I love You Lord.

[324] Anglican Church. Lambeth Conference, 1930

[325] (Mother) Teresa of Calcutta

[326] William Cowper (1731-1800)

[327] Traditional

Gospel Reading: Luke 23:13-25

Pilate summoned the chief priests and the rulers and the people, ^{14}and said to them, "You brought this man before me as one who corrupts *and* incites the people to rebellion. After examining Him before you, I have found no guilt in this Man regarding the charges which you make against Him. ^{15}No, nor has Herod, for he sent Him back to us; and indeed, He has done nothing to deserve death. ^{16}Therefore I will punish Him to teach Him a lesson and release Him." ^{17}Now he was obligated to release to them one prisoner at the Feast. ^{18}But they loudly shouted out all together, saying, "Away with this Man, and release Barabbas to us!" ^{19}He was one who had been thrown into prison for an insurrection that happened in the city, and for murder. ^{20}Pilate addressed them again, wanting to release Jesus, ^{21}but they kept shouting out, "Crucify, crucify Him!" ^{22}A third time he said to them, "Why, what wrong has He done? I have found no guilt no crime, no offense in Him *demanding* death; therefore I will punish Him to teach Him a lesson and release Him." ^{23}But they were insistent *and* unrelenting, demanding with loud voices that Jesus be crucified. And their voices *began* to prevail *and* accomplish their purpose. ^{24}Pilate pronounced sentence that their demand be granted. ^{25}And he released the man they were asking for who had been thrown into prison for insurrection and murder, but he handed over Jesus to their will.

 (44)

Jesus, I declare with Barabbas that the Cross You carried and hung on was meant for me. Though You did nothing to deserve death and lived a perfect life, You gave Yourself as an unblemished lamb for the atoning of my sins. The Righteous sacrificing His life for the unrighteous. I desire with all my heart to identify with You in Your suffering, death and resurrection. You are the Annointed One, the Christ, the Lamb who was slain, the Saviour and Redeemer. I give You thanks for Your endurance of unwarranted humiliation and for the weight of bearing all You did on the Cross. I praise Your holy Name and thank You for Your unfathomable love. I surrender my will, my mind, my emotions, my body, and my all to You, O King.

All praise and thanks to God the Father now be given, the Son, and Him who reigns with them in highest heaven; the one eternal God, whom earth and heaven adore; for thus it was, is now, and shall be ever more. Amen[328] Holy Spirit of God, You are a gracious and willing guest in every heart that is humble enough to receive You. Be present now with me and guide my prayer. For all the gracious privileges given to me this day past, I give You thanks. At Your invitation, and in the best way I know how, I have kept this day holy. For the books I have read and the music that uplifts, for this day's friendly interactions, and for the interior peace that has ruled my heart, I give You my heartfelt thanks. Grant, O heavenly Father, that the spiritual refreshment I have enjoyed may not be left behind and forgotten as I return tomorrow to the cycle of common tasks. O God, enable me so to discipline my will that in hours of stress I honestly seek after those things for which I have prayed in hours of peace. As I lie down to sleep, I commit all my dear ones to Your unsleeping care through Jesus Christ our Lord. Amen.[329]

O God of all power, You called from death the Great Pastor of the Sheep, the Lord Jesus, to comfort and defend the flock who He redeemed by the blood of the eternal testament. This was and is the Good News: He is alive forevermore. Increase the number of true preachers of this Gospel; lighten the hearts of the ignorant; relieve the pains of those who are afflicted, especially of those who suffer for the testimony of the truth. Please do this by the power of our Lord Jesus Christ.[330]

Remember, O Lord, Your Church, to deliver it from all evil and to perfect Her in Your love. Strengthen and preserve Her by Your Word and Sacraments. Enlarge Her borders, so that Your Gospel may be preached to all nations; and gather the faithful from all the ends of the earth into the Kingdom which You have prepared.[331]

Our Father who is in heaven, I pray for this country, that we might learn to appreciate the heritage that is ours. We all need to learn, in these challenging days, that to every human right there is attached a duty and to every privilege an obligation. Continue to teach me what freedom is: that it is not the right to do as I please, but the opportunity to be pleased to do what is right. Help me to learn how to trust in You as a Heavenly Father who loves me and who is concerned about what I do and what I am. Forgive me when I find it hard to trust and when I

[328] Martin Rinkart (1586-1649)

[329] Adapted from John Baillie, 1949

[330] John Knox, 1505-72

[331] Swedish Liturgy

am reluctant to put my faith in You. Give to me the faith to put my trust in You. May I learn, before I blunder. Lead me, show me what to do, and that it is possible for me to know Your will and to be a partner with You in doing what is right. This I ask in the Name of Christ, who never made a mistake and who is infinitely patient with those who seek to do His will. Amen.[332]

O Sacred Head, now wounded, with grief and shame weighed down; now scornfully surrounded with thorns, Your only crown. Mine, mine was the transgression, but Your's the deadly pain. What language shall I borrow to thank You, dearest friend, for this Your dying sorrow Your pity without end? O make me Yours forever and, should I fainting be, Lord, let me never, never outlive my love for You.[333] Lord, I love You. Stay with me through the night.

[332] Adapted from Peter Marshall (1902–67)

[333] Medieval Latin hymn

Gospel Reading: Luke 23:26-43

When they led Him away, they seized a man, Simon of Cyrene, who was coming in to the city from the country, and placed on him the cross to carry behind Jesus. ²⁷Following Him was a large crowd of the people, including women who were mourning and wailing for Him. ²⁸But Jesus, turning toward them, said, "Daughters of Jerusalem, do not weep for Me, but weep for yourselves and for your children. ²⁹For behold, the days are coming when they will say, 'Blessed are the barren, and the wombs that have not given birth, and the breasts that have never nursed.' ³⁰Then they will begin to say to the mountains, 'fall on us! And to the hills, 'cover us!' ³¹For if they do these things when the tree is green, what will happen when it is dry?" ³²Two others also, who were criminals, were being led away to be executed with Him. ³³When they came to the place called The Skull, there they crucified Him and the criminals, one on the right and one on the left. ³⁴And Jesus was saying, "Father, forgive them; for they do not know what they are doing." And they cast lots, dividing His clothes among themselves. ³⁵Now the people stood by, watching; but even the rulers ridiculed *and* sneered at Him, saying, "He saved others from death; let Him save Himself if He is the Christ of God, His Chosen One." ³⁶The soldiers also mocked Him, coming up to Him and cruelly offering Him sour wine, ³⁷and sarcastically saying, "If you are really the King of the Jews, save Yourself from death!" ³⁸Now there was also an inscription above Him: "This is the King of the Jews." ³⁹One of the criminals who had been hanged on a cross beside Him kept hurling abuse at Him, saying, "Are You not the Christ? Save Yourself and us from death!" ⁴⁰But the other one rebuked him, saying, "Do you not even fear God, since you are under the same sentence of condemnation? ⁴¹We *are suffering* justly, because we are getting what we deserve for what we have done; but this Man has done nothing wrong." ⁴²And he was saying, "Jesus, please remember me when You come into Your kingdom!" ⁴³ esus said to him, "I assure you *and* most solemnly say to you, today you will be with Me in Paradise.

☐ ☐ ☐ ☐ ☐ ☐ ☐ (45)

You are my God, the sole object of my love. For me, and such as me, You died to bear the horrific Cross, the nails, the spear; a thorny crown transpierced Your sacred brow. For me in torture You resigned Your breath, embraced me on the Cross, and saved me by Your death. And can these sufferings fail my heart to move? Such as then was, and is, Your love for me. Such was, and shall be still, my love for You. To You, Redeemer! Mercy's sacred spring! My God, my Father, Maker, and my King![334]

You are the Christ of God, King of the Jews and the King of kings. I am reminded that You were despised and rejected, a person of sorrows and not at all esteemed. You took up my infirmities and carried my sorrows. You were pierced for my transgressions and crushed for my iniquities. By Your wounds I am healed.[335] You were oppressed and afflicted yet You did not open Your mouth. You were led like a lamb to the slaughter. By oppression and judgment, You were taken away.[336] It is true that You did nothing to warrant suffering this unjust punishment but Your death made life possible for those who identify with You. You did not save Yourself from the pain and suffering, from the agony of sin-bearing but You saved me and others through Your finished work. You died on purpose and in love.

Deliver me, O Lord, from the foolishness of impatience. Let me not be in such a hurry to run on without You. It takes time to make things happen for Your Kingdom sake. I pray for transformations. It takes time to work out the kind of peace that will endure. O Lord, I need Your help to slow down, to take time to think, time to pray, and time to find and embrace Your unfolding plan for me. Give me the sense to walk in the way and at the pace You have foreordained for me. May all I do be for the good of others and for the glory of Your Name. Amen.[337]

O Lord, You have taught me that all my doings without love are worth nothing. Send Your Holy Spirit and pour into my heart that most excellent gift of love, the very bond of peace and all virtues, without which whosoever lives is counted dead before You. Grant me this for Your Son Jesus Christ's sake.[338] Loving God, look with mercy on Your servant who seeks in solitude and silence refreshment of soul and strengthening for service. Grant Your abundant blessing in the peace of Christ my Lord.[339]

---

[334] Alexander Pope, 1688-1744

[335] Isaiah 53:3-5

[336] Isaiah 53:7, 8

[337] Adapted from Peter Marshall (1902–67)

[338] Thomas Cranmer, 1489-1556

[339] The Daily Office

Reveal to me Your Word. Help me to understand that when I try to live without You, I am unable to live with myself. Convict me of the folly of walking against Your lights, that I may live longer and better. By the grace and mercy of Jesus Christ my Lord. Amen.[340]

God grant me the serenity, to accept the things I cannot change, the courage to change the things I can, and the wisdom to know the difference. Living one day at a time; enjoying one moment at a time; accepting hardship as a pathway to peace; taking, as you did, this sinful world as it is, not as I would have it; trusting that you will make all things right if I surrender to your will; that I may be reasonably happy in this life, and supremely happy with you in the next.[341]

Alas! And did my Saviour bleed? And did my Sovereign die? Would He devote that sacred head for a sinner such as I? Was it for sins that I have done, He goaned upon the tree? Amazing pity! Grace unknown! And love beyond degree! Well might the sin in darkness hide, and shut His glories in, when Christ, the mighty Maker died for humankind the creature's sin. Thus might I hide my blushing face while His dear Cross appears; dissolve my heart in thankfulness, and melt mine eyes to tears. But drops of grief can ne'er repay the debt of love I owe; here, Lord I give myself away, 'tis all that I can do.[342] I am Yours. I am safe in Your care. I worship You.

---

[340] Adapted from Peter Marshall (1902–67)

[341] Reinhold Niebuhr

[342] Isaac Watts (1674-1748)

Gospel Reading: Luke 23:44-56

It was now about noon, and darkness came over the whole land until 3:00 p.m., [45]because the sun was obscured; and the veil of the Holy of Holies of the temple was torn in two, from top to bottom. [46]And Jesus, crying out with a loud voice, said, "Father, into Your hands I commit My spirit!" Having said this, He breathed His last. [47]Now when the centurion saw what had taken place, he *began* praising *and* honouring God, saying, "Certainly this Man was innocent." [48]All the crowds who had gathered for this spectacle, when they saw what had happened, *began* to return to their homes, beating their breasts as a sign of mourning or repentance. [49]And all His acquaintances and the women who had accompanied Him from Galilee were standing at a distance, watching these things. [50]A man named Joseph, who was a member of the Council, a good and honourable man. [51]He had not consented to the Council's plan and action, *a man* from Arimathea - a city of the Jews, who was waiting for *and* expecting the kingdom of God. [52]This man went to Pilate and asked for the body of Jesus. [53]And after receiving permission he took it down and wrapped it in a linen burial cloth and laid Him in a tomb cut into the rock, where no one had yet been laid. [54]It was the day of preparation for the Sabbath, and the Sabbath was dawning. [55]Now the women who had come with Him from Galilee followed closely, and saw the tomb and how His body was laid. [56]Then they went back and prepared spices and ointments *and* sweet-smelling herbs. And on the Sabbath they rested in accordance with the commandment forbidding work.

☐ ☐ ☐ ☐ ☐ ☐ ☐ ☐ (46)

My soul magnifies You Lord, and my spirit rejoices in God my Saviour.[343] Oh, the depth of the riches of Your wisdom and knowledge O God! How unsearchable Your judgments, and Your paths beyond tracing out! Who has known Your mind O Lord? Or who has been Your counsellor? Who has ever given to You, that You should repay him? For from You and through You and to You are all things. To You, Lord, be the glory forever![344] Immortal Love, for ever full, forever flowing free, forever shared, forever whole, a never-ebbing sea! The letter fails, the systems fall, and every symbol wanes; the Spirit ever-brooding all, Eternal Love remains.[345]

---

[343] Luke 1.46-47 (New Revised Standard Version)

[344] Romans 11:33-36 (New international Version)

I praise You Triune God: Father, Son and Spirit, for the access I have to You through prayer. The curtain of the holy of holies has been torn, from top to bottom, and in the Name of Jesus Christ and by the blood He shed, I am able to approach You and offer myself as a living sacrifice to You. You did the same for me, but so much more. Into Your hands I commit every part of me. As I wait for Your Kingdom to come on earth as it is in heaven, use me, help me to be obedient to Your will and to put Your joy and overflowing love in my heart. Give me rest for my body tonight and awaken me with a sense of expectation for the adventure of tomorrow. Prepare my days for me and prepare me for all that must be done, for each person I will meet with, and for each occasion of decision and interaction. In Jesus Name, I pray.

This evening Lord I pray again in unison with others who have said: I have no idea where I am going. I do not see the road ahead of me. I cannot know for certain where it will end. Nor do I really know myself, and the fact that I think that I am following Your will does not mean that I am actually doing so. But I believe that the desire to please You does in fact please You. And I hope that I will never do anything apart from that desire. And I know that if I do this You will lead me by the right road though I may know nothing about it. Therefore I will trust You always. Though I may seem to be lost and in the shadow of death, I will not fear, for You are ever with me, and You will never leave me to face my perils alone.[346]

Holy God, to whose service I long ago dedicated my soul and life, I grieve and lament before You that I am still so prone to sin and so little inclined to obedience. I am so much attached to the pleasures of sense and so negligent of things spiritual. I am so prompt to gratify my body, so slow to nourish my soul. I am so greedy for present delight, so indifferent to lasting blessedness. I am so fond of idleness and so indisposed for labour. I find myself so soon at play, so late at prayer and so brisk in the service of self and so slack in the service of others. Dear Lord, I am so eager to get, yet so reluctant to give. I am so lofty in my profession, but so low in my practice. It is difficult to admit but I am so full of good intentions, and yet so backward to fulfill them. I am so severe with my neighbours, but indulgent with myself. Why is it that I am so eager to find fault, so resentful at being found with fault? I know I

[345] John Whittier (1807-1892)

[346] Thomas Merton, Thoughts on Solitude

am not so able for great tasks, but when am I so clearly discontented with small ones. As well I am so weak in adversity, so swollen and self-satisfied in prosperity. Lord I am so helpless apart from You, and yet so seldom willing to be bound to You. O merciful heart of God, grant me yet again Your forgiveness. Hear my sorrowful tale and in Your great mercy blot it out from the book of Your remembrance. Give me faith to lay hold of Your own holiness and to rejoice in the righteousness of Christ my Saviour. May I rest on His merits rather than on my own and may I more and more become conformed to Your likeness, my will becoming one with You in obedience. All this I ask for Your holy Name's sake. Amen.[347]

Lord, support and sustain my walk in Your way: where there is love and wisdom, there is neither fear nor ignorance; where there is patience and humility, there is neither anger nor annoyance; where there is poverty and joy, there is neither greed nor avarice; where there is peace and contemplation, there is neither worry nor restlessness; where there is mercy and prudence, there is neither excess nor harshness; this I know through Your Son, Jesus Christ my Lord.[348]

---

[347] Adapted from John Baillie, 1949

[348] Francis of Assisi, 1182-1226

Gospel Reading: Luke 24:1-12

But on the first day of the week, at early dawn, the women went to the tomb bringing the spices which they had prepared to finish anointing the body. ²And they found the large, circular stone rolled back from the tomb, ³but when they went inside, they did not find the body of the Lord Jesus. ⁴While they were perplexed *and* wondering about this, suddenly, two men in dazzling clothing stood near them; ⁵and as the women were terrified and were bowing their faces to the ground, the men said to them, "Why are you looking for the living One among the dead? ⁶He is not here, but has risen. Remember how He told you, while He was still in Galilee, ⁷saying that the Son of Man must be handed over to sinful men, and be crucified, and on the third day rise from death to life." ⁸And they remembered His words, ⁹and after returning from the tomb, they reported all these things to the eleven apostles and to all the rest. ¹⁰Now they were Mary Magdalene and Joanna, the wife of Chuza, Herod's steward, and Mary the *mother* of James; also the other women with them were telling these things to the apostles. ¹¹But their report seemed to them like idle talk *and* nonsense, and they would not believe them. ¹²But Peter got up and ran to the tomb. Stooping at the small entrance and looking in, he saw only the linen wrappings; and he went away, wondering about what had happened.

☐ ☐ ☐ ☐ ☐ ☐ ☐ ☐ (47)

Holy, holy, holy is the Lord God Almighty, who was, who is, and who is to come.³⁴⁹ To You who loved me and set me free from my sins with Your shed blood and who made Your redeemed ones a royal house to serve as the priests of God, to You be glory and dominion for ever!³⁵⁰

O Resurrected Lord Jesus, it is just as was said, the Son of Man must be delivered into the hands of sinful

men, be crucified and then on the third day be raised again. You have risen. You are risen, indeed! At the end of this day I recall the great price You paid as You took upon Yourself my sins and died for me – the righteous dying for the unrighteous. With refreshment, I also recall that You conquered death and are alive, forevermore. The same power that raised You from the dead now lives in me. I thank You for Your Spirit who guides and empowers. I bless you O

³⁴⁹ Revelation 4.8
³⁵⁰ Revelation 1.5, 6 (Revised English Bible)

Triune God, for the fact of Your power and victory over sin, death and the evil one. You are the conquering victor and You are the Giver of Life. Thank You for the gifts You have given. I will tell others of Your goodness, through Jesus Christ.

O Father in Heaven, before I become involved thinking through the routines of tomorrow, I pause to seek Your help. While I am getting more and more experienced in the ways of the world, I know all too little of the ways of God. Turn my wayward mind and heart to You. Forgive the faults and failures of the past day and set me free from these. Forgive, O Lord, my failure to apply the standards of conduct I demand of others. Forgive my slowness to see the good in others and to see the evil in myself. With others help me to be kind and humble, that Your will may be done in me, and through me. Help me to add value and to be a blessing to all those who cross my path tomorrow. Bless me this night with Your Spirit and help me to discharge my duties this week, faithfully and well. All this I beg for Jesus Christ's sake. Amen.[351]

If only I possessed the grace, good Jesus, to be utterly at one with You! Amidst all the variety of worldly things around me, the only thing I crave is unity with You. You are all my soul needs. Unite, dear friend of my heart, this unique soul of mine to Your perfect goodness. You are all mine; when shall I be all Yours? I realize that I don't need more of You; You need all of me. So, in the best way I know how, I yield myself fully to You. Lord Jesus, my beloved, be the magnet of my heart; clasp, press, unite me for ever to Your sacred heart. You have made me for Yourself; make me one with You.[352] Lord, help me to understand that You ain't gwine to let nuthin' come my way that You and me together can't handle.[353]

O Lord, my God, before whom all my pretenses fall away, You know my secret thoughts and my hidden fears, bless me this night with Your Spirit. Ever sensitive to hurting the feelings of others, may I also be sensitive to my grieving the Holy Spirit when I give myself to lesser loyalties and misspend my time and my energies. O God of Truth, who alone leads men and women into the truth that is freedom and joy, be my teacher as I seek to find the way of life in times that bewilder and challenge. Almighty God, Creator of all things, giver of every good and perfect gift, hear me at the end of this day as I seek

[351] Adapted from Peter Marshall (1902–67)

[352] Francis de Sales
[353] Source unknown

Your blessing upon my dreams and deliberations.[354]

Have Your own way, Lord! Have Your own way! You are the Potter, I am the clay. Mold me and make me after Your will, while I am waiting, yielded and still. Have Your own way, Lord! Have Your own way! Search me and try me, Master, today! Whiter than snow, Lord, wash me just now, as in Your presence humbly I bow. Have Your own way, Lord! Have Your own way! Wounded and weary, help me, I pray! Power, all power, surely is Yours! Touch me and heal me, Saviour divine. Have Your own way, Lord! Have Your own way! Hold o'er my being absolute sway! Fill with Your Spirit 'till all shall see Christ only, always, living in me.[355]

Into Your loving hands I commend my life. I love You Lord.

[354] Adapted from Peter Marshall (1902–67)

[355] Hymn by Adelaide Pollard

Gospel Reading: Luke 24:13-35

And then, that very day two of them were going to a village called Emmaus, which was about seven miles from Jerusalem. [14]And they were talking with each other about all these things which had taken place. [15]While they were talking and discussing it, Jesus Himself came up and *began* walking with them. [16]But their eyes were miraculously prevented from recognizing Him. [17]Then Jesus asked them, "What are you discussing with one another as you walk along?" And they stood still, looking brokenhearted. [18]One *of them*, named Cleopas, answered Him, "Are you the only stranger visiting Jerusalem who is unaware of the things which have happened here in these recent days?" [19]He asked, "What things?" And they replied, "The things about Jesus of Nazareth, who was a prophet powerful in deed and word in the sight of God and all the people, [20]and how the chief priests and our rulers handed Him over to be sentenced to death, and crucified Him. [21]But we were hoping that it was He who was going to redeem Israel *and* set our nation free. Indeed, besides all this, it is the third day since these things happened. [22]And also some of the women among us shocked us. They were at the tomb early in the morning, [23]and they did not find His body. Then they came back, saying that they had even seen a vision of angels who said that He was alive! [24]Some of those who were with us went to the tomb and found it just exactly as the women had said, but they did not see Him." [25]Then Jesus said to them, "O foolish men, and slow of heart to trust *and* believe in everything that the prophets have spoken! [26]Was it not necessary for the Christ to suffer these things and only then to enter His glory?" [27]Then beginning with Moses and throughout all the writings of the prophets, He explained *and* interpreted for them the things referring to Himself found in all the Scriptures. [28]Then they approached the village where they were going, and He acted as if He were going farther. [29]But they urged Him not to go on, saying, "Stay with us, because it is almost evening, and the day has just about ended." So He went inside to stay with them. [30]And it happened that as He reclined *at the table* with them, He took the bread and blessed it, and breaking it, He *began* giving it to them. [31]Then their eyes were suddenly opened by God and they clearly recognized Him; and He vanished from their sight. [32]They said to one another, "Were not our hearts burning within us while He was talking with us on the road and opening the Scriptures to us?" [33]They got up that very hour and went back to Jerusalem, and found the eleven apostles gathered together and those who were with them, [34]saying, "The Lord has really risen and has appeared to Simon Peter!" [35]They *began* describing in detail what had happened on the road, and how Jesus was recognized by them when He broke the bread.

☐ ☐ ☐ ☐ ☐ ☐ ☐ ☐ (48)

Lord God almighty, grant me a quiet night and a perfect end. My help is in the Name of the Lord who made heaven and earth. Jesus, You walk unseen with me throughout this journey of life. Today You were with me in every thought, every moment, each uncomfortable incident, each difficult conversation, each funny circumstance, each seemingly trivial and each apparently larger moment – You are ever and always with me. You are Prophet, Priest and King. You are Jesus of Nazareth. You are the Christ who suffered and then entered glory. I thank You for Your ever being present with me. I abide in You and You abide in me. Much happens along life's way as we walk together. Keep me from running ahead or following unwise paths, I look into Your face this evening and ask You to guide me with Your eyes. Speak to my heart, in and through the day to come. I ask You to fill me afresh with Your Spirit and to fully lead and direct my ways. May I be eyes wide-open to Your presence and Your transforming friendship with me, O Lord.

O Divine Father, whose mercy ever awaits those who return to You in true lowliness and contrition of heart, hear now one humble follower who needs Your help. Bravely I will set out in the morning for a new day but now I lie down ashamed and burdened with memories of things undone that ought to have been done and things done that ought not to have been done. Bring to me afresh, O God, Your healing and cleansing power, so that again I may lay hold of the salvation which You have offered to me through Jesus Christ my Lord.

For my deceitful heart and crooked thoughts, for barbed words spoken deliberately, for thoughtless words spoken hastily, for envious and prying eyes, for ears that rejoiced in iniquity and rejoiced not in the truth, for greedy hands, for wandering and loitering feet, for haughty looks. For all these have mercy upon me, O God. If I say that I have no sin, I deceive myself. Almighty God, Spirit of purity and grace, in asking Your forgiveness I cannot claim a right to be forgiven but only cast myself upon Your unbounded love. I can plead no merit nor can I can plead extenuating circumstances. I cannot plead the frailty of my nature and I cannot plead the force of the temptations I encounter. I cannot plead the persuasions of others who led me astray; I can only ask for forgiveness in Your Name and for the sake of Jesus Christ Your Son my Lord. Amen.[356]

Teach me, O God not to torture myself, not to make a martyr of myself through stifling reflection; but rather teach me to breathe deeply in faith, through Jesus, my Lord.[357] My heavenly Father, You order all things for my eternal good, mercifully enlighten my mind, and give me a firm and abiding trust in Your love and care. Silence my murmurings, quiet my fears, and dispel my doubts, that rising above my afflictions and my anxieties, I may rest on You, the rock of everlasting strength.[358] Lord Jesus put Your hands on my eyes, for then I too shall begin to look not at what is seen but at what is not seen.[359]

What good am I if I am like all the rest, if I just turn away, when I see how you're dressed, if I shut myself off so I can't hear you cry, what good am I? What good am I if I know and don't do, if I see and don't say, if I look right through you, if I turn a deaf ear to the thundering' sky, what good am I? What good am I while you softly weep and I hear in my head what you say in your sleep, and I freeze in the moment like the rest who don't try, what good am I? What good am I if I say foolish things and I laugh in the face of what sorrow brings and I just turn my back while you silently die, what good am I?[360] Dear Lord make me useful.

O LORD, teach me to number my days that I may apply my heart to wisdom. God help me to respond to need and to Your promptings in my life. Teach me to listen. Time is short, and no one knows how little time he or she has left. May I be found using my given time, talents and strength wisely. Break to me these days the bread of life. I love You Lord. Be with me through the night and ready me for the adventure of tomorrow.

[356] Adapted from John Baillie, 1949

[357] Soren Kierkegaard, 1813-55

[358] New Church Book of Worship, 1876

[359] Origen, c.185-c.254

[360] Bob Dylan, 1989 Special Rider Music

Gospel Reading: Luke 24:36-53

While they were talking about this, Jesus Himself suddenly stood among them and said to them, "Peace be to you." [37]But they were startled and terrified and thought that they were seeing a spirit. [38]And He said, "Why are you troubled, and why are doubts rising in your hearts? [39]Look at the marks in My hands and My feet, and see that it is I Myself. Touch Me and see; a spirit does not have flesh and bones, as you see that I have." [40]After saying this, He showed them His hands and His feet. [41]While they still did not believe it because of their joy and amazement, He asked them, "Do you have anything here to eat?" [42]They gave Him a piece of broiled fish, [43]and He took it and ate it in front of them. [44]Then He said to them, "This is what I told you while I was still with you, everything which has been written about Me in the Law of Moses and the writings of the Prophets and the Psalms must be fulfilled." [45]Then He opened their minds to help them understand the Scriptures, [46]and said, "And so it is written, that the Christ would suffer and rise from the dead on the third day, [47]and that repentance necessary for forgiveness of sins would be preached in His name to all the nations, beginning from Jerusalem. [48]You are witnesses of these things. [49]Listen carefully: I am sending the Promise of My Father, the Holy Spirit, upon you; but you are to remain in the city of Jerusalem until you are fully equipped with power from on high." [50]Then He led them out as far as Bethany, and lifted up His hands and blessed them. [51]While He was blessing them, He left them and was taken up into heaven. [52]And they worshiped Him and returned to Jerusalem with great joy, fully understanding that He lives and that He is the Son of God; [53]and they were continually in the temple blessing *and* praising God.

 (49)

I receive Your peace tonight O Prince of Peace. This peace is not the peace offered by the world but is Your shalom. You are my Peace. In your presence there is peace. You have fulfilled all that was written in Moses, in the Prophets and in the Psalms.

You are the historical and contemporary Jesus Christ, my Lord and Saviour. Clothe me this night, with power from on high, for the days to come so that I might be a witness to all the promise of the Good News. Thank You for blessing my life – each and every day. Give to me Your joy as my strength. Make Your face to shine on me and may Your praise be constantly on my lips and expressed in my life – lived for You, by You, and overflowing into the lives of others. Make me an instrument of Your peace, in Jesus Name, I pray.

Lord, since You exist, I exist. Since You are beautiful, I am beautiful. Since You are good, I am good. By my existence I honour You. By my beauty I glorify You. By my goodness I love You. Lord, through Your power all things were made. Through Your wisdom all things are governed. Through Your grace all things are sustained. Give me power to serve You, wisdom to discern Your laws, and grace to obey at all times.[361] Batter my heart, three-person'd God, for you. O'erthrow me and bend Your force to break, blow, burn, and make me new.[362]

I bless You, O most holy God, for the unfathomable love whereby You have ordained that spirit with Spirit can meet and that I, a weak and erring mortal, should have this ready access to the heart of Him who moves the stars. With regret and true compunction of heart I acknowledge before You the gross and selfish

thoughts that I so often allow to enter my mind and to influence my deeds. I confess, O God-- that often I let my mind wander down unclean and forbidden ways. I confess that often I deceive myself as to where my plain duty lies and that often, too often, by concealing my real motives, I pretend to be better than I am. Lord my honesty is only a matter of policy and my affection for my friends is only a refined form of caring for myself. I confess that often my shortcomings are due to nothing more than cowardice. I agree that often I do good deeds only that they may be seen by others so they will think well of me, and I shun evil ones only because I fear I may be found out and rejected. I am beginning to understand that maturity in You is living an undefended life. O holy One, let the fire of Your love enter my heart, and burn up all this coil of meanness and hypocrisy, and make my heart as the heart of a little child. I give up the false self I've created and ask that You would nurture the authentic me. Give me grace, O God, to pray with pure and sincere desire for all those with whom I have had to do this day. Let me remember now my friends with love and my enemies with forgiveness, entrusting them all, as I now entrust my own soul and body, to Your

[361] Edmund of Abingdon, c.1180-1240

[362] Holy Sonnets, 14, Donne, John. Poems of John Donne. vol I. E. K. Chambers, ed. London: Lawrence & Bullen, 1896. 165

protecting care, through Jesus Christ. Amen.[363]

Lord, give me seeing faith, then my work will never be monotonous. I will ever find joy in humouring the fancies and gratifying the wishes of all poor sufferers. Lord make me appreciative of the dignity of my high vocation, and its many responsibilities. Never permit me to disgrace it by giving way to coldness, unkindness, or impatience. And, O God, bear with my faults, looking only to my intention, which is to love and serve You in the person of each of Your poor, vulnerable, sick and hurting loved ones. Lord, increase my faith, bless my efforts and work, now and for evermore.[364]

Now let the heavens be joyful, let earth her song begin; let the round world keep triumph and all that is therein; invisible and visible, their notes let all things blend, for Christ the Lord has risen, my Joy that has no end.[365] Lord, heavenly Father, in whom is the fullness of light and wisdom, enlighten my mind by Your Holy Spirit, and give me grace to receive Your Word with reverence and humility, without which no one can understand Your truth; for Jesus Christ's sake. Amen.[366]

[363] Adapted from John Baillie, 1949

[364] (Mother) Teresa of Calcutta (Her daily prayer)

[365] John of Damascus

[366] John Calvin

Prayer Prompts and Lists[367]

Immediate family members

_____

_____

_____

_____

_____

_____

Extended family members

_____

_____

_____

_____

_____

_____

Neighbours

_____

_____

_____

_____

_____

_____

[367]Church House Publishings (UK) – *Time to Pray*, Baker Books – *Seeking God's Face*, and Faith Alive Christian Resources (USA) – *Prayers of the People* are three of numerous references that have helped me to develop the lists found in Part 10.

Friends and families of friends

_____

_____

_____

_____

_____

_____

Friends, family, and others with special needs

_____

_____

_____

_____

_____

_____

Co-workers, colleagues, fellow students

_____

_____

_____

_____

_____

_____

Churches (Local and Universal)

_____
_____
_____
_____
_____
_____

Pastor(s), priest(s) and their families

_____
_____
_____
_____
_____
_____

Congregation/Parish leaders and their families

_____
_____
_____
_____
_____
_____

Church Body and their particular needs

_____
_____
_____
_____
_____
_____
_____

Particular ministries

_____
_____
_____
_____
_____
_____

Particular events

_____
_____
_____
_____
_____
_____

Particular prayer requests

_____

_____

_____

_____

_____

_____

_____

_____

_____

_____

_____

Personal needs

_____

_____

_____

_____

_____

_____

_____

_____

_____

_____

_____

_____

- International Workers/Missionaries
- The universal Church of Christ
- All those who lead the Church
- Leaders of the Nations
- The natural world and the resources of the Earth
- All who are in any kind of need
- The media and the arts
- Farmers and Fishers
- Commerce and industry
- Those whose work is unfulfilling, stressful or fraught with danger
- All who are unemployed
- Asia and its countries
- God's royal priesthood, that they may be empowered by the Spirit
- Those who wait on God, that they may find renewal
- The earth, for productivity and for fruitful harvests
- All who are struggling with broken relationships
- The saints on earth, that they may live as citizens of heaven
- All people, that they may hear and believe the Word of God
- All who fear the winter months
- All sovereigns and political leaders, that they may imitate the righteous rule of Christ
- All who grieve or wait with the dying
- Africa and its countries
- Homeless people
- Families with young children
- All who are lonely
- All who are near to death
- All who are facing loss
- The people of God, that they may proclaim the risen Lord
- God's creation, that the peoples of the earth may meet their responsibility to care
- Those in despair and darkness, that they may find the hope and light of Christ
- Those in fear of death, that they may find faith through the resurrection

- Prisoners and captives
- Prisoners, refuges and homeless people
- Our homes, families, friends, and all whom we love
- Those whose time is spent caring for others
- Those who are close to death
- Those who have lost hope
- The worship of the Church
- The Church, especially in places of conflict
- The Holy Land, for peace and justice and reconciliation
- Refugees and asylum seekers
- Immigrant families
- Europe and its countries

- Those living in poverty or under oppression
- Local government, community leaders
- All who provide local services
- Schools, colleges, apprenticeship programs and universities
- Emergency and rescue organizations
- The Queen, members of parliaments, legislatures, councils and the armed forces
- Peace and justice in the world
- Those who work for reconciliation
- All whose lives are devastated by war and civil strife
- Oceania Area and its countries
- Those who are enslaved
- The unity of the Church
- Peace in the world
- The healing of the sick
- The revelation of Christ to those from whom His glory is hidden
- All who travel
- Those preparing for spiritual rites of passage

Let us then with confidence draw near to the throne of grace, that we may receive mercy and find grace to help in time of need.[368] Cast your burden on the Lord, and he will sustain you; he will never permit the righteous to be moved.[369]

[368] Hebrews 4:16

[369] Psalm 55:22

- Those who are mislead by the false gods of this present age
- All who are hungry
- The persecuted Church
- The oppressed and colonized people of the world
- North and Central America and those countries
- All who are sick in body, mind, or spirit
- Those in the midst of famine or disaster
- Victims of abuse and violence, intolerance and prejudice
- Those who are bereaved
- All who work in the medical, health care and healing professions
- The social services workers
- Victims and perpetrators of crime
- The work of aid and relief agencies throughout the world
- Special States, Dependent Territories, Limited Recognition States
- My immediate family members
- My extended family members
- My neighbours
- My friends and families of friends
- Friends, family, and others with special needs
- My co-workers, colleagues, fellow students
- Churches (Local and Universal)
- Pastor(s), priest(s) and their families
- Church congregations
- Particular ministries:
- Particular region of world:
- Particular event(s):
- My personal needs:
- Missionaries and international workers
- Mid-Eastern countries
- Spiritual renewal and a deep sense of repentence
- Readiness to give a reason for the hope within us
- The flourishing of Christ's church everywhere
- Our capacity to serve the common good
- South America and its countries
- Those serving in leadership

- All who work in the criminal justice and correction systems
- Indigenous peoples who are at the margins of society
- Racial reconciliation
- Emerging generation
- Employment of those seeking work
- Those seeking asylum, refuge status, and escape from life-threatening places
- Deep missional identity in local churches
- Creative new conversation, environment and sustainability technologies
- Prisoners of conscience and emboldened advocates for justice
- Capacity to see and savour the wonder, beauty and complexity of creation
- Rights, best interests, and well-being of children, especially vulnerable children
- Effective teaching and preaching of God's Word
- Equipping for those working in the public arena, through elected roles
- Wise stewardship of physical resources
- Grace of asking forgiveness and for the boldness to confront wrong doing
- Muscians and artists who colour our world and fill our hearts with delight
- Eyes to see God's work in the world
- Members of gangs, crime communities, and tribes at war
- Those who are reminding us that we only have one planet, so we should smarten up
- A renewal of interest and commitment to serve the common good
- Those working in the news media
- Those trapped in prostitution, the sex industry; for drug dealers, and vice-advocates
- Deep involvement of local churches in the needs around them

- Deep and growing gratitude for the cross of Jesus Christ and His healing promises
- Safety of those who work in dangerous places or with dangerous substances
- The three or four countries in the world that might otherwise be ignored, even unknown
- Our stepped up efforts to reduce, reuse, and recyle
- Downfall of Satan and his despicable cohorts
- Uncovering of false and useless idols in our hearts
- For the lonely, abandoned, disenfranchised, cheated and exploited
- Fellowship with the risen Jesus Christ and for an abiding wonder at His sacrifice
- A deep awakening to the Gospel message amongst the apparently cold and disaffected
- A yearning to know God and the diligence to seek Him
- Those looking for forgiveness

- Church leaders

CONCERNS FOR PETITION, SUPPLICATION, & INTERCESSION

For Creation

- Harvest
- Natural resources
- Environmental concerns
- Natural disasters
- Seasonal weather
- Restoration of planet
- Consumption
- Renewal of resources
- The sky, land, and waters
- Stewardship of all created things

For the World

- Places and people at war
- Circumstances of injustice
- Experiences of hunger
- Experiences of disease
- Circumstances of racial strife
- World governments
- International crises
- International relief organizations
- International organizations

- Senior and elder statespersons
- Peace-makers

Sustainable Development Goals

- Eradication of extreme poverty and hunger
- Achievement of universal primary education
- Promotion of gender equality and empowerment of women
- Reduction of child mortality
- Improved maternal health
- Combatting of HIV/AIDS, malaria and other diseases
- Ensuring environmental sustainability
- Development of global partnerships for development

For the Nation

- Courts and judges
- National leaders
- Elections
- Military personnel
- Advocates for justice and peace
- Leaders of the public service

- National business and social sector leaders
- Indigenous leaders and peoples
- Circumstances of injustice and poverty
- Circumstances of hunger and homelessness
- New and establishing immigrants

For the Province/State/Local Community

- Provincial/State leaders
- Justice leaders, workers & the whole justice sector
- Social services leaders, workers & the whole social services sector
- Health care leaders, workers & the whole health care sector
- Education leaders, workers & the whole education sector
- Civil servants
- Business sector, social sector and service organizations
- Local governments and public services
- Reduction of homelessness & poverty: Issues and situations

- Reducton of racial strife
- Schools, hospitals and human services institutions
- Fire, police, ambulance, utilities workers and services

For the Church Universal

- Persecuted Church and persecuted persons
- Christians working in unfriendly places
- Unity of the Church
- Benevolent work
- Work with women and children in difficult circumstances
- Holiness of the Church
- International workers and mission agencies
- Christian education: schools, colleges, universities and seminaries
- Denominations
- Denominational missions & programs
- Christian emergency and relief organizations
- Para-church organizations

For the Local Congregations/Parishes

- Pastor(s), priest(s), deacon(s), and minister(s)
- Bishop(s), superintendent(s), president(s) of denomination(s)
- Boards, councils, synods, committees and governing bodies
- Elders and other lay leaders
- Congregation/Parish staff members
- Teachers
- Caretaker/custodian(s)
- Receptionist(s)
- Stewards of congregation/parish finances
- Musicians, artists and technical support people
- Short term international service participants
- All members and adherents in community witness
- Local outreach and service to community
- Unity of congregation(s)
- New congregations/parishes and those involved

- Ethnic churches
- Churches working with particularly vulnerable people and people groups

For Those with Special Needs

- Those who suffer with physical illness, and those who care for them
- Those who suffer with mental illness, and those who care for them
- Those who are elderly and infirm, and those who care for them
- Those who have suffered abuse, and those who support them
- Those who suffer with addiction, and those who support them
- Those who mourn the death of love one(s), and those who minister to them
- Those who are lonely, and those who care for them
- Those who are homeless, and those who care for them
- Those who are victims of crime, and those who support them
- Those who needs cannot be spoken
- Those who are facing temptations
- Those who live a single persons
- Those who are about to be married or who are newly married
- Those who celebrate their wedding anniversaries
- Those who struggle with marital difficulties
- Those who are divorced or separated
- Those who are widowed
- Those who are separated from spouses and family because of circumstances
- Those whose sexuality is a source of pain
- Those who have felt unloved because of their sexuality or the hateful acts of others
- Those who celebrate the birth of a child
- Those who long for children
- Those who have adopted a child or children
- Those who are adopted

- Those who care for young children
- Those who care for troubled or high risk adolescents
- Those who care for elderly or needy parents
- Those who are just starting school
- Those who are struggling with peer pressure
- Those who are tying to choose an educational or career path
- Those who are leaving home
- Those who are unemployed or underemployed
- Those who work in business and industry
- Those who work in homemaking
- Those who work in health care
- Those who work in education
- Those who work in agriculture
- Those who work in government
- Those who work in service to others
- Those who are beginning a new career
- Those who struggle with their work or their boss(es)
- Those who are seeking new or different work
- Those who are retired or anticipating retirement
- Those who celebrate baptism
- Those who celebrate a renewed faith commitment or profession of faith
- Those who struggle with doubts
- Those who are persecuted for their faith/Faith
- Those who seek spiritual renewal
- Those with family members and friends who do not yet have faith
- Those who travel
- Those who are enjoying leisure and rest
- Those who travel to be present to worship with others
- Those who are new members of faith communities